100 DAYS PRAYERS TO WAKE UP YOUR LAZARUS

THE TRANSFORMING POWER OF
ACTIVELY WAITING ON GOD

PRAYER M. MADUEKE

ISBN: 979-8648047518

Published by Prayer Publications.

Printed in the United States of America.

4 Free Ebooks

In order to say a 'Thank You' for purchasing *100 Days Prayers to Wake Up Your Lazarus*, I offer these books to you in appreciation. Click or type madueke.com/free-gift in your browser.

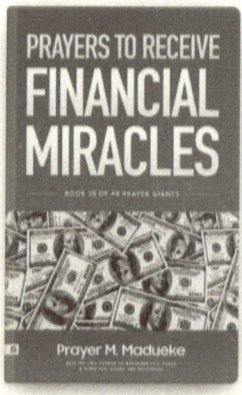

Message from the Author

I want to see you succeed, grow, and break free from negativity and obstacles. My hope is for you to thrive, unaffected by negative influences and challenging situations. Because of that, please permit me to introduce two courses that I believe passionately will help you:

1. To break the evil altars and powers of your father's house, The role of altars in the realm of existence is very key because altars are meeting places between the physical and the spiritual, between the visible and the invisible.

   Unless a man cuts off the evil flow from the power of his father's house, he will not fulfil his destiny. **Click here** to learn more about **my course** on how to tear down unholy altars and close the enemy's entryways into your life!

2. To help you seamlessly break iron-like problems, illness, delayed marriage, poverty, or any long-standing battle.

   Discover **the transformative power of Christian fasting and prayer**. Remember, Matthew 17:21 teaches us, *"But this kind of demon does not go out except by prayer and* *fasting."* Ready to overcome your struggles? <u>Click here</u> to learn more about this course.

Embrace the journey ahead with faith, for through prayer, fasting, and the dismantling of evil altars, you shall unlock the doors to spiritual liberation and divine breakthrough. May your path be illuminated by His grace as you walk towards a life free from bondage.

If you're seeing this from the physical copy, type the link: <u>madueke.com/courses</u> in your browser to view all the courses on my website.

Prayer Madueke
CHRISTIAN AUTHOR

Christian Counselling

We were created for a greater purpose than only survival and God wants us to live a full life.

If you need prayer or counselling, or if you have any other inquiries, please visit the counselling page on my website to know when I will be available for a phone call.

Click or type links.madueke.com/counselling in your browser.

Let's Connect on Youtube ▶

Join me on my YouTube channel, "Prayer M. Madueke," where I share powerful insights, guidance, and prayers for spiritual breakthroughs.

Subscribe today to unlock the secrets of the Kingdom and embrace an abundant life. Let's grow together!

Click or type **links.madueke.com/youtube** in your browser.

Table of Contents

CHAPTER ONE

WHO IS YOUR DESTINY?

"Then said his disciples, Lord, if he sleep, he shall do well." (John 11:12)

Your destiny is something to which you as a person or thing is destined. It is like a fortune, predetermined course of events often held to be an irresistible power or agency. It can be linked to somebody, another person, member of your family or a friend. It is time for you to start praying to meet your destiny helper, one assigned to assist you fulfil God's purpose here on earth and to make heaven at last. If you allow such person, your destiny helper to die, you may suffer long or even achieve nothing in life. Therefore, the question is, who is your destiny? Your Destiny is the most important person in your life, the only son of your parents. He is the heir in your father's house, the future of your family and its breadwinner. He is the beloved of God and the only male voice in your father's house, the hope and the joy of your future existence. Any sickness against Destiny can affect the whole family and can replace joy with sorrow. It can cause big problems in a whole city.

Your Destiny can be any person or thing that is very precious to you. Your Destiny can be your living healthy parents, child or relation who is ready to assist you in life. Your Destiny can be a determined friend who is ever ready to help you in life. He can be a person planted by God somewhere to be of help to your present predicament. Your Destiny can be your wife or husband who means a lot to your well-being. Your Destiny can be any part of your eyes, leg, brain, your reproductive organ. It can be your academic life, business, marriage or health.

Your Destiny may be your movement into a particular place, a simple re-location to a city, just a simple crossover to another nation. Your Destiny may be given admission into a particular school not just into any school.

Your Destiny may be your ministry, your pastor who is about to quarrel with you or you are about to quarrel with. Your Destiny may be just a transfer out of your helpers or from whom your helpers are located. Your Destiny may be the baby you aborted seven years ago or you are about to abort. It may be an opportunity you are about to miss.

You may even conspire against your God-given Destiny. Your Destiny may be your house help who you have treated like a slave. Your Destiny may be your half-brother/sister who you refused to help out of his/her problem or who you refused to see through his or her school. Your Destiny may be your driver, servant or junior in your office.

Your Destiny can be one of your neglected children, a despised daughter or son. You can reject your Destiny, dismiss your Destiny and insult your Destiny without knowing. You may see your Destiny as your enemy and treat your enemies as your Destiny. You may sell your Destiny without knowing it. You may kill your Destiny with your own hand. "Who is your Destiny"? Your Destiny may be the woman whose hand you are rejecting in marriage. You may hate your Destiny without reasons. If you are destined to live in Ghana but you are living in Nigeria and you are about to die in Nigeria, you have missed your Destiny. If you are supposed to marry Christopher but you get married to Sunday, you have missed your Destiny. If you are supposed to be an international figure but you are giving testimony because you are a local government provost during your last stay on earth, you have failed in life, and at the same time, you have missed your Destiny.

Your Destiny is anything, person or place that makes difficult things easy in life. It is a divine deposit or provision that makes the impossible, possible for your life. Your Destiny is a divine deposit or provision that guides your career to the right destination. It is the glory formed by God to make things easy for you. Your Destiny is the divine helper assigned to assist you in life. It is the divinely provided help, which, if you miss you cannot get quality help in life.

DO NOT MISS YOUR DESTINY!

Everyone is born with a Destiny. If your Destiny is handed over to your enemy the day you were born, you are in trouble, but if your Destiny is in Christ, no grave can contain you.

> *"Before I formed thee in the belly, I knew thee; and before thou camest forth out of the womb I sanctified thee, and I ordained thee a prophet unto the nations."*
> *(Jeremiah 1:5)*

THINGS THAT CAN HAPPEN TO YOUR DESTINY

1. Your Destiny can be sick

2. Your Destiny can be caged

3. Your Destiny can be paralyzed

4. Your Destiny can be evil affected

5. Your Destiny can be damaged

6. Your Destiny can be cast down

7. Your Destiny can be locked up

8. Your Destiny can be demoted

9. Your Destiny can be stolen

10. Your Destiny can be executed

11. Your Destiny can be completely removed

12. Your Destiny can be hindered

13. Your Destiny can be cursed

14. Your Destiny can be buried

15. The light of your Destiny can be deemed

16. Your Destiny can be stagnated

17. Your Destiny can expire

18. Your Destiny can be sunk in water

19.   Your Destiny can be prevented from being born

20.   Your Destiny can be born with struggle

21.   Your Destiny can be arrested

22.   Your Destiny can be diverted

23.   Your Destiny can be weak

24.   Your Destiny can be detained in prison

25.   Your Destiny can be scattered

26.   Your Destiny can be under molestation

27.   Your Destiny can be surrounded by satanic agents

28.   Your Destiny can be harvested by enemies

29.   Your Destiny can be seized by Satan

30.   Your Destiny may be hospitalized

31.   Your Destiny may be defeated

32.   Your Destiny may be condemned

33.   Your Destiny may be confused

34.   Your Destiny may be old

35.   Your Destiny may be amputated

36.   Your Destiny can be killed

37.   Your Destiny can be imprisoned.

A person can kill his Destiny by refusing to repent and accept Jesus Christ as his Lord and personal Savior. A Christian can kill his Destiny by refusing to fight his life's battle.

"Submit yourselves therefore to God. Resist the devil, and he will flee from you." (James 4:7)

Ignorant parents can kill their children's Destiny by evil dedications of their children to idols, cults and other evil groups. Witches and wizard use any available weapon to destroy people's Destiny.

"And it came to pass, as we went to prayer, a certain damsel possessed with a spirit of divination met us, which brought her masters much gain by soothsaying: The same followed Paul and us, and cried, saying, these men are the servants of the most-high God, which shew unto us the way of salvation. And this did she many days. But Paul, being grieved, turned and said to the spirit, I command thee in the

name of Jesus Christ to come out of her. And he came out the same hour." (Acts 16:16-18)

Abel's Destiny died because of household wickedness.

"And Cain talked with Abel his brother: and it came to pass, when they were in the field, that Cain rose up against Abel his brother, and slew him." (Genesis 4:8)

His own brother for no just cause murdered him. Household wickedness is destroying many Destinies' today. Joseph faced extreme attack from household wickedness that nearly amputated his Destiny. Moses, a great man of God, was badly attacked by household wickedness. Miriam and Aaron spoke against his Destiny before all Israel.

"And Miriam and Aaron spake against Moses because of the Ethiopian woman whom he had married: for he had married an Ethiopian woman.

And they said, Hath the LORD indeed spoken only by Moses? hath he not spoken also by us? And the LORD heard it. (Now the man Moses was very meek, above all the men which were upon the face of the earth.) And the LORD spake suddenly unto Moses, and unto Aaron, and unto Miriam, Come out ye three unto the tabernacle of the congregation. And they three came out. And the LORD came down in the pillar of the cloud, and stood in the door of the tabernacle, and called Aaron and Miriam: and they both came forth. And he said, hear now my words: If there be a prophet among you, I the LORD will make myself known unto him in a vision, and will speak unto him in a dream. My servant Moses is not so, who is faithful in all mine house. With him will I speak mouth to mouth, even apparently, and not in dark speeches; and the similitude of the LORD shall he behold: wherefore then were ye not afraid to speak against my servant Moses? And the anger of the LORD was kindled against them; and he departed." (Number 12:1-9)

The Destiny of our Savior Jesus was also attacked by a household enemy (Luke 4:14-32, 7:23, 30, 8:37).

"And his sisters, are they not all with us? Whence then hath this all these things? And they were offended in him. But Jesus said unto them, A prophet is not without honor, save in his own country, and in his own house. And he did not many mighty works there because of their unbelief." (Matthew 13:56-58)

Herod beheaded the Destiny of John the Baptist through sudden death and sent him to the grave before his time.

"For Herod had laid hold on John, and bound him, and put him in prison for Herodias' sake, his Brother Philip's wife. For John said unto him, it is not lawful for thee to have her. And when he would have put him to death, he feared the multitude, because they counted him as a prophet. But when Herod's birthday was kept, the daughter of Herodias danced before

them, and pleased Herod. Whereupon he promised with an oath to give her whatsoever she would ask. And she, being before instructed of her mother, said, Give me here John Baptist's head in a charger. And the king was sorry: nevertheless, for the oath's sake, and them which sat with him at meat, he commanded it to be given her. And he sent, and beheaded John in the prison. And his head was brought in a charger, and given to the damsel: and she brought it to her mother." (Matthew 14:3-11)

A certain beggar's Destiny was arrested and made useless with the weapon of poor desire.

"And desiring to be fed with the crumbs which fell from the rich man's table: moreover, the dogs came and licked his sores. And it came to pass, that the beggar died, and was carried by the angels into Abraham's bosom: the rich man also died, and was buried;" (Luke 16:21-22)

POWERS THAT CAN ATTACK YOUR DESTINY

1. Spiritual armed robbers, sex in dreams etc.

2. Ancestral powers.

3. Evil habit (difficult to stop)

4. Envious enemies.

5. Poison.

6. Bewitchment.

7. Demonic prayers.

8. Evil initiations or evil summons.

9. Unexplainable diseases without medical diagnosis.

10. Foundational or inherited poverty.

11. Excessive anger.

12. Evil marks.

13. Witchcraft manipulation.

14. Lust.

15. Unexplainable persistent problems.

16. Wickedness.

17. Shedding innocent blood (abortion etc.).

18. Forsaking God.

19. Sexual immorality-adultery/sexual perversion.

20. Drunkenness.

21. Unfriendly friends.

22. Wrong choice.

23. Evil diversion.

24. Evil dedication.

25. Marine powers.

26. Iniquity.

27. Death.

28. Wrong marriage.

CHAPTER TWO

THE RISEN DESTINY

---

1. Joseph

"And Jacob dwelt in the land wherein his father was a stranger, in the land of Canaan. These are the generations of Jacob. Joseph, being seventeen years old, was feeding the flock with his brethren; and the lad was with the sons of Bilhah, and with the sons of Zilpah, his father's wives: and Joseph brought unto his father their evil report. Now Israel loved Joseph more than all his children, because he was the son of his old age: and he made him a coat of many colors. And when his brethren saw that their father loved him more than all his brethren, they hated him, and could not speak peaceably unto him. And Joseph

dreamed a dream, and he told it his brethren: and they hated him yet the more. And he said unto them, Hear, I pray you, this dream which I have dreamed: For, behold, we were binding sheaves in the field, and, lo, my sheaf arose, and also stood upright; and, behold, your sheaves stood round about, and made obeisance to my sheaf. And his brethren said to him, Shalt thou indeed reign over us? or shalt thou indeed have dominion over us? And they hated him yet the more for his dreams, and for his words. And he dreamed yet another dream, and told it his brethren, and said, Behold, I have dreamed a dream more; and, behold, the sun and the moon and the eleven stars made obeisance to me. And he told it to his father, and to his brethren: and his father rebuked him, and said unto him, what is this dream that thou hast dreamed? Shall I and thy mother and thy brethren indeed come to bow down ourselves to thee to the earth? And his brethren envied him; but his father observed the saying. And his brethren went to feed their father's flock in Shechem. And Israel said unto Joseph, do not thy brethren feed the flock in Shechem?

come, and I will send thee unto them. And he said to
him, here am I. And he said to   him, Go, I pray
thee, see whether it be well with thy brethren, and
well with the flocks; and bring me word again. So, he
sent him out of the vale of Hebron, and he came to
Shechem. And a certain man found him, and, behold,
he was wandering in the field: and the man asked
him, saying, what seekest thou? And he said, I seek
my brethren: tell me, I pray thee, where they feed their
flocks. And the man said, they are departed hence; for
I heard them say, let us go to Dothan. And Joseph
went after his brethren, and found them in Dothan."
(Genesis 37:1-17)

He had a dream concerning his great Destiny. At seventeen years old, the Lord, through a dream, showed him his great Destiny while he was feeding his father's flock. His brothers hated him because he was a man of great dream.

"And he said unto them, Hear, I pray you, this dream
which I have dreamed: For, behold, we were binding

sheaves in the field, and, lo, my sheaf arose, and also stood upright; and, behold, your sheaves stood round about, and made obeisance to my sheaf. And his brethren said to him, Shalt thou indeed reign over us? or shalt thou indeed have dominion over us? And they hated him yet the more for his dreams, and for his words." (Genesis 37:6-8)

Joseph's Destiny appeared like a sheaf that was bowed to by other sheaves in his father's house. In his second dream, the Destiny of his father and his mother were humbled before his Destiny together with the Destiny of his eleven brothers.

"And he dreamed yet another dream, and told it his brethren, and said, Behold, I have dreamed a dream more; and, behold, the sun and the moon and the eleven stars made obeisance to me. And he told it to his father, and to his brethren: and his father rebuked him, and said unto him, what is this dream that thou hast dreamed? Shall I and thy mother and thy brethren indeed come to bow down ourselves to thee

to the earth? And his brethren envied him; but his
father observed the saying". (Genesis 37:9-11)

Everybody is born with a Destiny but some Destinies are greater than others. The brothers of Joseph did everything humanly possible to eliminate the Destiny of Joseph but they failed. They all hated him, envied him and sold him to a strange land but the Lord was with him everywhere. Joseph's relationship with God was maintained inside and outside his father's house. He bluntly refused and vehemently rejected any offer that would separate him from his God. All the sins that were released to divert, destroy or bury his Destiny were not given a moment's opportunity to succeed.

He was demoted and reduced to an ordinary slave but he remained faithfulness both at home and abroad. He was promoted to an overseer and was given an opportunity to share with his master in his matrimonial bed but he chose to deny himself temporary enjoyment that would dim the light of his Destiny. He chose to please God instead of self and man.

"And it came to pass after these things, that his master's wife cast her eyes upon Joseph; and she said, lie with me. wotteth not what is with me in the house, and he hath committed all that he hath to my hand; There is none greater in this house than I; neither hath he kept back anything from me but thee, because thou art his wife: how then can I do this great wickedness, and sin against God? And it came to pass, as she spake to Joseph Day by day that he hearkened not unto her, to lie by her, or to be with her." (Genesis 39:7-10)

His decision landed him in prison and his Destiny was under great attack. However, while in prison, his leadership Destiny arose and interpreted the dreams of his fellow prisoners

"And they dreamed a dream both of them, each man his dream in one night, each man according to the interpretation of his dream, the butler and the baker of the king of Egypt, which were bound in the prison. And Joseph came in unto them in the morning, and

looked upon them, and, behold, they were sad. And he asked Pharaoh's officers that were with him in the ward of his Lord's house, saying, wherefore look ye so sadly today? And they said unto him, we have dreamed a dream, and there is no interpreter of it. And Joseph said unto them, do not interpretations belong to God? Tell me them, I pray you. And the chief butler told his dream to Joseph, and said to him, in my dream, behold, a vine was before me; And in the vine were three branches: and it was as though it budded, and her blossoms shot forth; and the clusters thereof brought forth ripe grapes: And Pharaoh's cup was in my hand: and I took the grapes, and pressed them into Pharaoh's cup, and I gave the cup into Pharaoh's hand. And Joseph said unto him, this is the interpretation of it: The three branches are three days: Yet within three days shall Pharaoh lift up thine head, and restore thee unto thy place: and thou shalt deliver Pharaoh's cup into his hand, after the former manner when thou wast his butler. But think on me when it shall be well with thee, and shew kindness, I pray thee, unto me, and make mention of me unto

Pharaoh, and bring me out of this house: For indeed I was stolen away out of the land of the Hebrews: and here also have I done nothing that they should put me into the dungeon. When the chief baker saw that the interpretation was good, he said unto Joseph, I also was in my dream, and, behold, I had three white baskets on my head: And in the uppermost basket there was of all manner of bake meats for Pharaoh; and the birds did eat them out of the basket upon my head. And Joseph answered and said, this is the interpretation thereof: The three baskets are three days: Yet within three days shall Pharaoh lift up thy head from off thee, and shall hang thee on a tree; and the birds shall eat thy flesh from off thee. And it came to pass the third day, which was Pharaoh's birthday that he made a feast unto all his servants: and he lifted up the head of the chief butler and of the chief baker among his servants. And he restored the chief butler unto his butlership again; and he gave the cup into Pharaoh's hand: But he hanged the chief baker: as Joseph had interpreted to them. Yet did not the

chief butler remember Joseph, but forgot him."
(Genesis 40:5-23)

Pharaoh, the greatest man of his time, sent for him for dream interpretation.

"Then Pharaoh sent and called Joseph, and they brought him hastily out of the dungeon: and he shaved himself, and changed his raiment, and came in unto Pharaoh. And Pharaoh said unto Joseph, I have dreamed a dream, and there is none that can interpret it: and I have heard say of thee, that thou canst understand a dream to interpret it. And Joseph answered Pharaoh, saying, it is not in me: God shall

.give Pharaoh an answer of peace." (Genesis 41:14-16)

Joseph interpreted pharaoh's dream and his Destiny was promoted above all his enemies within and outside that nation.

"And the thing was good in the eyes of Pharaoh, and in the eyes of all his servants. And Pharaoh said unto his servants, can we find such a one as this is, a man in whom the Spirit of God is? And Pharaoh said unto Joseph, Forasmuch as God hath shewed thee all this, there is none so discreet and wise as thou art: Thou shalt be over my house, and according unto thy word shall all my people be ruled: only in the throne will I be greater than thou. And Pharaoh said unto Joseph, See, I have set thee over all the land of Egypt. And Pharaoh took off his ring from his hand, and put it upon Joseph's hand, and arrayed him in vestures of fine linen, and put a gold chain about his neck; And he made him to ride in the second chariot which he had; and they cried before him, Bow the knee: and he made him ruler over all the land of Egypt." (Genesis 41:37-43)

Joseph needed his God-given wisdom to make the Egyptian government very rich and his Destiny was highly elevated.

"And in the seven plenteous years the earth brought forth by handfuls. And he gathered up all the food of the seven years, which were in the land of Egypt, and laid up the food in the cities: the food of the field, which was round about every city, laid he up in the same. And Joseph gathered corn as the sand of the sea, very much, until he left numbering; for it was without number. And unto Joseph were born two sons before the years of famine came, which Asenath the daughter of Potipherah priest of On bare unto him. And Joseph called the name of the firstborn Manasseh: For God, said he, hath made me forget all my toil, and all my father's house. And the name of the second called he Ephraim: For God hath caused me to be fruitful in the land of my affliction. And the seven years of plenteousness, which was in the land of Egypt, were ended. And the seven years of dearth began to come, according as Joseph had said: and the dearth was in all lands; but in all the land of Egypt there was bread. And when all the land of Egypt was famished, the people cried to Pharaoh for bread: and

Pharaoh said unto all the Egyptians, Go unto Joseph; what he saith to you, do. And the famine was over all the face of the earth: And Joseph opened all the storehouses, and sold unto the Egyptians; and the famine waxed sore in the land of Egypt. And all countries came into Egypt to Joseph for to buy corn; because that the famine was so sore in all lands. (Genesis 41:47-57)

Finally, the Destiny of Joseph that was despised, hated, cast down and forgotten prevailed over all other sinful Destinies of his father's house and they all bowed down to him.

"And when Joseph came home, they brought him the present which was in their hand into the house, and bowed themselves to him to the earth." (Genesis 43:26)

God takes the final decision and upholds it, not your enemies; the gang ups of the witches and wizards cannot stop the Destiny of a righteous, militant, prayerful and determined believer.

"The LORD maketh poor, and maketh rich: he bringeth low, and lifteth up. He raiseth up the poor out of the dust, and lifteth up the beggar from the dunghill, to set them among princes, and to make them inherit the throne of glory: for the pillars of the earth are the LORD'S, and he hath set the world upon them. He will keep the feet of his saints, and the wicked shall be silent in darkness; for by strength shall no man prevail. The adversaries of the LORD shall be broken to pieces; out of heaven shall he thunder upon them: the LORD shall judge the ends of the earth; and he shall give strength unto his king, and exalt the horn of his anointed." (1 Samuel 2:7-10)

Pharaoh gave command to destroy the Destiny of all the male children in Egypt of the seed of the Hebrews but Moses survived it. Some powers can prevent Destiny from being born. Some

Destinies die at birth and some die after birth. The parents of Moses, including her sister, fought to preserve the Destiny of Moses (Exodus 1:15-22. 2:1-10).

Moses' identification with God and his people promoted, preserved and caused his Destiny to prevail over his enemies.

"By faith Moses, when he was born, was hid three months of his parents, because they saw he was a proper child; and they were not afraid of the king's commandment. By faith Moses, when he was come to years, refused to be called the son of Pharaoh's daughter; Choosing rather to suffer affliction with the people of God, than to enjoy the pleasures of sin for a season; Esteeming the reproach of Christ greater riches than the treasures in Egypt: for he had respect unto the recompence of the reward. By faith he forsook Egypt, not fearing the wrath of the king: for he endured, as seeing him who is invisible. Through faith he kept the Passover, and the sprinkling of blood, lest he that destroyed the firstborn should touch them. By faith they passed through the red sea

as by dry land: which the Egyptians assaying to do
were drowned." (Hebrews 11:23-29)

He ran away from Egypt when he knew that the powers of the
Egyptians were determined to bury his Destiny (Exodus 2:15-
25, 3:7-10).

Unlike Laban and Jacob, Moses and his father-in-law separated
in perfect peace and agreement (Exodus 4:18-23). Moses
answered God's call, and he allowed God to use him to gather
all the persecuted elders of Israel and delivered God's message
to them (Exodus 4:27-31. 6:21-27, 7:6,7,20. 8:1,5-15, 20-24,
9:13-33, 12:29-36).

He boldly approached Pharaoh whom Satan used to capture
and enslave the people of God.

"Now these are the names of the children of Israel,
which came into Egypt; every man and his household
came with Jacob. Issachar, Zebulun, and Benjamin,
and it came to pass, because the midwives feared
God, that he made them houses. And Pharaoh

charged all his people, saying, every son that is born ye shall cast into the river, and every daughter ye shall save alive." (Exodus 5:1, 3, 21, 23)

Moses also bluntly refused to compromise with Pharaoh and at the end of the battle; God used him to deliver all the Destinies of the children of Israel from the hands of the stubborn king of the Egyptians.

"And it came to pass, that at midnight the LORD smote all the firstborn in the land of Egypt, from the firstborn of Pharaoh that sat on his throne unto the firstborn of the captive that was in the dungeon; and all the firstborn of cattle. And Pharaoh rose up in the night, he, and all his servants, and all the Egyptians; and there was a great cry in Egypt; for there was not a house where there was not one dead. And he called for Moses and Aaron by night, and said, Rise up, and get you forth from among my people, both ye and the children of Israel; and go, serve the LORD, as ye have said. (Exodus 12:29-31)

DEAD CHILD

This young girl died in the hand of a merciless spirit of premature death. Her Destiny was destroyed both spiritually and physically but she had a man of faith as a father. Her father was able to secure an appointment with Jesus. This man was a ruler but his ruler ship was not over spiritual powers, so he approached the man who had power and dominion over every kingdom and the dead Destiny of his daughter was called back to life.

"Now when Jesus saw great multitudes about him, he gave commandment to depart unto the other side. And a certain scribe came, and said unto him, Master, I will follow thee whithersoever thou goest. And when he was entered into a ship, his disciples followed him. And, behold, there arose a great tempest in the sea, insomuch that the ship was covered with the waves: but he was asleep. And his

disciples came to him, and awoke him, saying, Lord,

save us: we perish. (Matthew 9:18, 19, 23-25)

THE ONLY SON

This dead man was the only son in this family, and he was an orphan because his mother was a widow. There were many people in that city but they could not fight to stop the killer of the young men in their community. When Jesus saw this company of people, being led by Mr. Death, he had compassion on this widow. On the other side of the city gate was Jesus, and his company. It was life versus death but Jesus won the battle.

"Now when he came nigh to the gate of the city, behold, there was a dead man carried out, the only son of his mother, and she was a widow: and much people of the city was with her. And when the Lord saw her, he had compassion on her, and said unto her, Weep not. And he came and touched the bier: and they that bare him stood still. And he said, young man, I say unto thee, Arise. And he that was dead sat up, and began to speak. And he delivered him to his mother." (Luke 7:12-15)

There is a risen Destiny in the bible days. Those who know their God shall be strong and do exploits.

> *"And such as do wickedly against the covenant shall he corrupt by flatteries: but the people that do know their God shall be strong, and do exploits. (Daniel 11:32)*

2. Dorcas

This devoted woman, a disciple at Joppa, was attacked with a sickness until she died. The disciples at Joppa took her and made her lie in an upper chamber. They believed in God and his servants, so they sent for Peter. The prayers of Peter touched her Destiny and she was revived.

> *"Now there was at Joppa a certain disciple named Tabitha, which by interpretation is called Dorcas: this woman was full of good works and alms deeds*

which she did. And it came to pass in those days, that she was sick, and died: whom when they had washed, they laid her in an upper chamber. And forasmuch as Lydda was nigh to Joppa, and the disciples had heard that Peter was there, they sent unto him two men, desiring him that he would not delay to come to them. Then Peter arose and went with them. When he was come, they brought him into the upper chamber: and all the widows stood by him weeping, and shewing the coats and garments which Dorcas made, while she was with them. But Peter put them all forth, and kneeled down, and prayed; and turning him to the body said, Tabitha, arise. And she opened her eyes: and when she saw Peter, she sat up." (Acts 9:36-40)

3. Eutychus

This young man's Destiny was targeted and killed right inside the church at a midnight sermon. The enemy used the weapon of deep sleep to destroy his Destiny. He sank down with sleep, fell down from the third loft, and was taken up dead. Satan himself removed his Destiny but fortunately, his Destiny was revived again.

> "And there sat in a window a certain young man named Eutychus, being fallen into a deep sleep: and as Paul was long preaching, he sunk down with sleep, and fell down from the third loft, and was taken up dead. And Paul went down, and fell on him, and embracing him said, Trouble not yourselves; for his life is in him. When he therefore was come and had broken bread, and eaten, and talked a long while, even till break of day, so he departed. And they brought the young man alive, and were not a little comforted. (Act 20:9-12)

4. Destiny

This Destiny of our text was dead and buried for four days but his sisters contacted the Resurrection and Life. When you have contact with Jesus, your Destiny will simply leave the graveyard and your destiny will be fulfilled.

"Jesus said unto her, I am the resurrection, and the life: he that believeth in me, though he were dead, yet shall he live: And said, where have ye laid him? They said unto him, Lord, come and see. Jesus said, Take ye away the stone. Martha, the sister of him that was dead, saith unto him, Lord, by this time he stinketh: for he hath been dead four days. And when he thus had spoken, he cried with a loud voice, Destiny, come forth. And he that was dead came forth, bound hand and foot with grave clothes: and his face was bound about with a napkin. Jesus saith unto them, lose him, and let him go." (John 11:25, 34, 39, 43, 44)

Your Destiny can arise if you believe in Jesus. If you confess your sin and repent genuinely, no power can keep your Destiny in bondage. People are wicked, but you are more wicked if you refuse to repent, confess your sins and forsake them.

"For if we sin willfully after that we have received the knowledge of the truth, there remaineth no more sacrifice for sins, but a certain fearful looking for of judgment and fiery indignation, which shall devour the adversaries. He that despised Moses' law died without mercy under two or three witnesses: Of how much sorer punishment, suppose ye, shall he be thought worthy, who hath trodden underfoot the Son of God, and hath counted the blood of the covenant, wherewith he was sanctified, an unholy thing, and hath done despite unto the Spirit of grace? For we know him that hath said, Vengeance belongeth unto me, I will recompense, saith the Lord. And again, The Lord shall judge his people. It is a fearful thing to fall into the hands of the living God." (Hebrews 10:26-31)

Those who are foolish repent today and return to their vomit daily. They keep away from sin when they are having problems and return to it as soon as God solves the problems. The bible commands that every man should repent, confess his sins, forsake them and live a holy life. Be a consistent Christian. Do not think that you can mock God or deceive Him. Your thoughts in the next twenty years (even to the end of your life) are exposed before God. You are the only person holding your Destiny. If you first repent, confess and forsake your sins, the graves of your Destiny will submit to the divine voice and your Destiny shall arise.

CHAPTER THREE

YOUR DESTINY SHALL ARISE!

"Jesus saith unto her, thy brother shall rise again."

(John 11:23)

What is the grave of your Destiny? Where is the grave of your Destiny? What is the evidence to show that your Destiny is captured?

The grave of your Destiny is the place where your problem started. It is the place where the enemy buried your Destiny. Nevertheless, what is the evidence to show that your Destiny is captured, killed, destroyed etc.?

EVIDENCES

- Failure to listen to good advice until costly mistakes are made

- Unexplainable depression

- Overwhelming confusion

- Unexplainable problem

- Unexplainable rising and falling

- Uncontrollable sexual desire

- Repeated financial misappropriation

- Deep-rooted habits

- Fear of failure

- Late marriage or breakage of marriage engagement

- Constant dream of water or losing vital items in the dream

- Having sex or any other evil relationship in the dream especially with an unknown person.

- Loss of memory or vital information when you need it most.

- Inability to take good decisions on time

- Having repeated problems or being a victim every time

- Backwardness in every venture

- Immediate loss of intelligence, good things, or great opportunity

- Always facing problems, restlessness

- Falling and rising in spiritual matters

- Inability to keep good decisions you have taken

- Dreaming of a particular place, e.g., your place of birth, old school, houses or cities you lived but left long ago

- Wearing old school uniforms

- Taking an exam, you have taken and passed before

- Inability to finish any good thing on time, in peace and with joy

- Being pursued in the dream by masquerades, serpents, etc.

- Having blockage at the edge of miracles

- Recording major failures in a particular house, in an office, or an area

- Having an incurable disease

- Having a better past either, spiritually or physically

- Having a weakness inside after a long period of good (rest) sleep

- Having a sleepless night

- When good doors get closed and refuse to open again

- Having interrupted joy

- Being hated and frustrated

- Meeting only people who may show willingness to help you but will not be able to do so

- Watching helplessly and seeing your lifetime investment collapsing

- Having physical but spiritually dead children who are without a future

- Facing many enemies or fighting many (battles) problems

- Quarrelling with people that are ordained to help you or separating with beloved ones

- Finding it difficult to pray and almost impossible to (fight) pray for a long time.

- One good thing in our study today is what Christ Himself said in John 11:23:

"Jesus said unto her, thy brother shall rise again".

If you agree with Jesus, your Destiny shall arise again, no matter how far or long the enemies have held it. Only believe and you will see a miracle.

"Jesus saith unto her, Said I not unto thee, that, if thou wouldest believe, thou shouldest see the glory of God? (John 11:40)

Those who believed God by faith in the bible days were not disappointed. They all had testimonies and their Destinies rose from the dead.

"By faith the walls of Jericho fell down, after they were compassed about seven days. By faith the harlot Rahab perished not with them that believed not, when she had received the spies with peace. And what shall I more say? for the time would fail me to tell of Gedeon, and of Barak, and of Samson, and of Jephthae David also, and Samuel, and of the prophets: Who through faith subdued kingdoms, wrought righteousness, obtained promises, stopped the mouths of lions, Quenched the violence of fire, escaped the edge of the sword, out of weakness were made strong, waxed valiant in fight, turned to flight the armies of the aliens. Women received their dead raised to life again: and others were tortured, not accepting deliverance; that they might obtain a better resurrection: (Hebrews 11:30-35)

When true born-again people pray, God answers. Noah prayed and God saved him and his family from the flood. Abraham prayed and God gave him Isaac and made him the father of all nations. Moses prayed and God destroyed all the armies of the Egyptians that were after his life and ministry. Elisha asked for a double portion and received it, and Jesus say to you.

> *"Ask, and it shall be given you; seek, and ye shall find; knock, and it shall be opened unto you: For every one that asketh receiveth; and he that seeketh findeth; and to him that knocketh it shall be opened. (Matthew 7:7, 8)*

Hezekiah prayed and received healing and health for 15 years. Jabez prayed and God enlarged his coast and granted him all that which he requested. Daniel prayed and God gave him an open vision. All her enemies were destroyed because of her prayers. Job prayed for his enemies and God restored all that he lost seven times.

"Therefore, take unto you now seven bullocks and seven rams, and go to my servant Job, and offer up for yourselves a burnt offering; and my servant Job shall pray for you: for him will I accept: lest I deal with you after your folly, in that ye have not spoken of me the thing which is right, like my servant Job. And the LORD turned the captivity of Job, when he prayed for his friends: the LORD gave Job twice as much as he had before. Then came there unto him all his brethren, and all his sisters, and all they that had been of his acquaintance before, and did eat bread with him in his house: and they bemoaned him, and comforted him over all the evil that the LORD had brought upon him: every man also gave him a piece of money, and everyone an earring of gold. So, the LORD blessed the latter end of Job more than his beginning: for he had fourteen thousand sheep, and six thousand camels, and a thousand yoke of oxen, and a thousand she asses. He had also seven sons and three daughters. And he called the name of the first, Jemima; and the name of the second, Kezia; and the name of the third, Kerenhappuch. And in all the land

were no women found so fair as the daughters of Job:
and their father gave them inheritance among their
brethren. After this lived Job an hundred and forty
years, and saw his sons, and his sons' sons, even four
generations. So, Job died, being old and full of days.
(Job 42:8, 10-17)

"Thou renewest thy witnesses against me, and
increasest thine indignation upon me; changes and
war are against me. (Job 10:17)

Blind Bartimaeus prayed and God opened his eyes after about 40 years of blindness. He recovered his Destiny.

If ordinary prayer cannot resurrect your Destiny, you can fast. Moses fasted for 40 days and 40 nights without food.

Joshua and the elders of Israel fasted. Elijah fasted to overthrow the evil kingdom of his generation. Jehoshaphat and all Judah fasted and God took over the battle from them.

Joel called for a fast; we need to fast to recover our Destiny from the hands of our stubborn enemies.

> *"Lament like a virgin girded with sackcloth for the husband of her youth. The meat offering and the drink offering is cut off from the house of the LORD; the priests, the LORD'S ministers, mourn. Sanctify ye a fast, call a solemn assembly, gather the elders and all the inhabitants of the land into the house of the LORD your God, and cry unto the LORD, O LORD, to thee will I cry: for the fire hath devoured the pastures of the wilderness, and the flame hath burned all the trees of the field. (Joel 1:8, 9, 14, 19)*

Jesus fasted for 40 days and 40 nights.

> *"Then was Jesus led up of the Spirit into the wilderness to be tempted of the devil. And when he had fasted forty days and forty nights, he was afterward an hungred. (Matthew 4:1, 2)*

Our Destiny may need just a simple prayer to be awakened. To some, their Destiny may need some hours of fasting to be awakened.

To some still, they may need more than 40 days. It depends on how far your Destiny has been taken. Occult people are fasting for 100 days to get power, some more or less depending on how far they want to go with Satan. Satanic technology is advancing and spiritual Christians may need more than 70 days to fit in. The prayer points in this book will guide you even if you want to go into hundred days of fasting or more.

I am believing God that you will be guided by the holy Ghost to take the right decision so as to pray until your Destiny rises again.

"Jesus saith unto her, thy brother shall rise again. And whosoever liveth and believeth in me shall never die. Believest thou this? And when he thus had spoken, he cried with a loud voice, Destiny, come forth. And he that was dead came forth, bound hand and foot grave clothes: and his face was bound about

with a napkin. Jesus saith unto them, loose him, and let him go." (John 11:23, 26, 43, 44)

The light that is going to give you deliverance has come and already, those who can see, have seen the glory of God upon you.

You have heard the testimonies of other people; your own testimony has come already. With this book in your hand, it is your time to give your testimony. You have attended other people's wedding; your own wedding is at hand and it is going to be great. You have entered other people's car; you will begin to enter your own personal car. Whatever you are not able to do before; you will begin to do them. If you are blind, your healing has come. Your entire problem must go. You are going to give testimony.

If you put the light of God in this book, into practice it will bring deliverance to many people. To start right, you must first be born again, confess every sin, forsake every sin, be holy and have faith in God. Believe that all things are possible to them that believe.

I have prayed for you, and as you pray your own prayer, you will be delivered, spiritually, physically, financially, socially, academically, materially, martially and mentally from every bondage and captivity. I am waiting to hear your testimony. God bless you in Jesus' name, Amen. Your Destiny shall arise. I thought you would say. Amen.

A friend of mine bought a cursed land in the city of Lagos, Nigeria, from an occultic man. Immediately he started the building, all his sources of income were affected. His pharmaceutical company collapsed and his building project was brought to a standstill. Everything about him entered into a crisis. He was advised against taking a loan from the bank but he decided against it and took the loan that amounted to millions of naira.

Yet, his business went ill that his shop almost got empty and his customers ran away from him. He could no longer pay the monthly interest he agreed with the bank.

The bank was getting ready to take over the uncompleted two-story building. In the midst of all the trouble, his children's school fees became a big problem. His property owner was also making trouble. Everything was against him. In the middle of that crisis, his first son, about 9 years old, started fasting and praying. He prayed for seven days before his parents decided to go into a spiritual battle to sort themselves out.

This wonderful husband and wife prayed and fasted for a very long time. On their ninetieth day of fasting, their heavens opened, unknown to them.

"Oh, that thou wouldest rend the heavens, that thou wouldest come down, that the mountains might flow down at thy presence," (Isaiah 64:1)

By the end of their prayers, it was as if nothing had happened. A few months later, an unknown person, somebody from the USA who they had never seen in life approached the man and asked for his quotation to supply some drugs to their firm.

In the end, he started supplying drugs to the firm and the profit he made in the few supplies he made restored all that he had lost for years, paid his debts in the bank, completed his building, restructured his business life, and made him a better Christian.

When I saw him last, his wife and their first daughter just came back from the USA for a short time of holiday.

He fought his battle and today he is a property owner, a director of a pharmaceutical firm and great minister in his local assembly. You can decide to marry if you want. Your loss can be recovered even to a double portion; anything you want to do is possible. You can make it. A miracle awaits everybody who can look up to God and pray with righteousness.

> *"Elias was a man subject to like passions as we are and he prayed earnestly that it might not rain: and it rained not on the earth by the space of three years and six months. And he prayed again, and the heaven gave rain, and the earth brought forth her fruit."*
> *(James 5:17-18)*

CHAPTER FOUR

WARFARE PRAYER POINTS

"Arise, shine; for thy light is come, and the glory of the LORD is risen upon thee." Isaiah 60:1

Those who were brought up in African villages can understand the reference in this introduction. The children of Israel were cattle rearers. They kept cattle, so the Lord used the language they would understand very well. They were shepherds for their trade was to feed cattle (Genesis 4:32-34)

When a shepherd takes his flock to the bush and ties them to a tree with ropes in their necks, the flock will be limited according to the length of the ropes. Normally, as the shepherd makes a move to leave the place, the flocks will cry after him but running towards the shepherd, the ropes will stop them.

In an attempt to free themselves from the limitation of the ropes, they may try the north side, east side; west and south sides but the ropes will still hold them under limitation and bondage.

After consuming all the green pasture in the four cardinal points of the bush, they will lie down in a place with full knowledge that there is no more hope of escape. Even if the owner comes back to release them, they will still believe that, deliverance is no more possible. The owner may beat them, shout on them but they may not believe that there is freedom because they have tried all day long without solution.

> *"And Simon answering said unto him, Master, we have toiled all the night, and have taken nothing: nevertheless, at thy word I will let down the net. And when they had this done, they inclosed a great multitude of fishes: and their net brake." (Luke 5:5, 6)*

That was the condition of the children of Israel in the days of Isaiah.

"Awake, awake; put on thy strength, O Zion; put on thy beautiful garments, O Jerusalem, the holy city: for henceforth there shall no more come into thee the uncircumcised and the unclean. Shake thyself from the dust; arise, and sit down, O Jerusalem: loose thyself from the bands of thy neck, O captive daughter of Zion." (Isaiah 52:1, 2)

For good seventy years, they were in captivity to the people of Babylon and other heathen nations. They did everything possible to be freed but all proved abortive. At the end, they all settled down in Babylon and completely said, good-bye to deliverance and freedom.

Just one faithful day God spoke through Isaiah. According to the amplified bible, God spoke to them, thus:

"Awake, Awake, put on your strength, o Zion; put on your beautiful garments, o Jerusalem, the holy city; for henceforth

there shall no more come into you the circumcised and the unclean, shake yourself from the dust arise, sit (elect in a dignified place), o Jerusalem; loose yourself from the bonds of your neck, o captive daughter of Zion."

For seventy good years, many deceivers who promised them freedom deceived them. So many of them died in their bondage. They saw everybody who talks about deliverance as a deceiver, including Isaiah the prophet.

> *"Awake, awake, put on strength, O arm of the LORD; awake, as in the ancient days, in the generations of old. Art thou not it that hath cut Rahab, and wounded the dragon? Awake, awake, stand up, O Jerusalem, which hast drunk at the hand of the LORD the cup of his fury; thou hast drunken the dregs of the cup of trembling, and wrung them out." (Isaiah 51:9, 17)*

You have read many books, prayed many prayers, visited great prophets and preachers without solution. You have attended many Christian programmes, retreats, crusades and many great seminars and yet your problem persisted. In the past, as an unbeliever, you might have tried many ways but you were deceived. You might have decided that you will not even believe God but I want to prove you wrong. God is still talking to you.

DAY 1

Esther 4:1, 8, 15-17

Oh Lord, Awake My Destiny

1. My Cain, you shall not kill my Abel, in the name of Jesus.

2. Oh Lord, save my Noah from the flood of destruction, in the name of Jesus.

3. You my childless Abraham, spiritually or physically, die by fire, in the name of Jesus.

4. Holy Ghost fire, take me away from Sodom and Gomorrah, in the name of Jesus.

5. Any hand of Abimelech, male or female upon my life, dry up--in the name of Jesus.

6. Oh Lord, the water in my bottle is finished; take me to the well of the water of life, in the name of Jesus.

7. Father Lord, open my blind eyes to see your divine provision, in the name of Jesus.

8. Any barrenness in my Sarah and Rebecca, disappear in the name of Jesus.

9. All you envious philistines against my Isaac, scatter, in the name of Jesus.

10. The philistine shall not choose the well of water against me, in the name of Jesus.

11. My Esau shall not destroy the Jacob of my destiny, in the name of Jesus.

12. My Jacob shall not die under slavery, in the name of Jesus.

13. Any power attacking the prayers of my Destiny, fall down and die in the name of Jesus.

14. Make your personal request.

15. Pray in the Spirit for a very long time.

DAY 2

Esther 4:1, 8, 15-17

Oh Lord, Awake My Destiny

5.   You spirit of fear, tormenting my Jacob because of Esau, die immediately, in the name of Jesus.

6.   Oh Lord, let my Jacob find favor to return to his promised land, in the name of Jesus.

7.   By fire, by fire, oh Lord, change my name, in the name of Jesus.

8.   Any power that wants to kill my Joseph, fail woefully, in the name of Jesus.

9.   Let my Egyptian bondage break into pieces, in the name of Jesus.

10.   Any spirit of confusion upon my Moses, die by fire, in the name of Jesus.

11.   My Israelite shall not suffer the plagues of the Egyptians, in the name of Jesus.

12.   All the success of my pharaoh, be converted to failures, in the name of Jesus.

13.   You, my Moses, confront your Pharaoh with boldness, in the name of Jesus.

14.   From today, I refuse to see the Egyptian army, in the name of Jesus.

15.   You my Israel, you shall not lack water in the wilderness, in the name of Jesus.

16.   Let the armies of the Amalekites, ready to confront me be wiped out, in the name of Jesus.

17.   The widows of my life, you shall not be oppressed, in the name of Jesus.

18.   You my raiment, taken as a pledge by the wicked, be released by force, in the name of Jesus.

19.   Pray in the Spirit for a very long time.

DAY 3

Exodus 24:15-18

Oh Lord, Awake my Destiny

1. Oh Lord, as you showed Moses your glory, show me your glory in this programme, in the name of Jesus.

2. You my leprosy, disappear by fire, in the name of Jesus.

3. Oh Lord, put fire on my prayer altar, in the name of Jesus.

4. Let the Miriam of our congregation be delivered, in the name of Jesus.

5. My Moses shall not be afflicted with pestilence, in the name of Jesus.

6. You my Dathan, Korah and Abiram, die without mercy, in the name of Jesus.

7. All you powers, speaking against my Moses, be buried alive, in the name of Jesus.

8. Any Balaam on any altar, making sacrifices against my Israel, die, in the name of Jesus.

9. My Moses shall not die outside the Promised Land, in the name of Jesus.

10. My Israelite shall not murmur, rebel or underestimate God, in the name of Jesus.

11. Oh Lord, let my Moses see the Promised Land and live long there, in the name of Jesus.

12. I command every curse placed upon my Destiny to expire by force, in the name of Jesus.

13. Blood of Jesus, flow into the grave of my dead Destiny and empower him, in the name of Jesus.

14. Lord Jesus, breathe your life saving power into my dead Destiny, in the name of Jesus.

15. Any instrument that Cain has used to kill my Destiny, I burn you to ashes, in the name of Jesus.

DAY 4

Esther 4:1, 8, 15-17

Oh Lord, Awake My Destiny

1. Oh Lord, write your covenant son the table of my heart, in the name of Jesus.

2. Achan shall not put my Israel in trouble, in the name of Jesus.

3. Any hand of oppression from the Midianites upon my Israel, dry up, in the name of Jesus.

4. You the Samson of my Manoah, appear, in the name of Jesus.

5. Oh Lord, give my thirsty Samson the water of life, in the name of Jesus.

6. My Samson shall not die with the Philistines, in the name of Jesus.

7. You my Hannah, you shall not die without Samuel, in the name of Jesus.

8. You my Samuel, hear the voice of God in the house of God, in the name of Jesus.

9. My Eli will not have ungodly and useless children, in the name of Jesus.

10. Any spirit of Nahash demanding my right eye, scatter with your armies, in the name of Jesus.

11. Any evil plan against my David by Saul, be revealed by fire, in the name of Jesus.

12. O Lord, reject my Saul and remove him from the throne, in the name of Jesus.

13. Every witchcraft weapon against my Destiny, kill your owner by force, in the name of Jesus.

14. Every Goliath of my Destiny, I hit your four head with the stones of David, in the name of Jesus.

15. Father Lord, empower my Destiny to begin to call upon your name, in the name of Jesus.

DAY 5

Esther 4:1, 8, 15-17

Oh Lord, Awake My Destiny

1. Oh Lord, help me to recover all my loss as you did for David, in the name of Jesus.

2. All the philistines looking for my David, receive blindness, in the name of Jesus.

3. Every effort of the philistines against my David, be wasted, in the name of Jesus.

4. The conspiracy and counsel of my Ahitophel shall backfire, in the name of Jesus.

5. Oh Lord, frustrate all the strange women assigned to destroy my Solomon, in the name of Jesus.

6. Oh Lord that visited Solomon in the dream, I am waiting for you, visit me, in the name of Jesus.

7. The food of the old prophet shall not destroy my anointing and life, in the name of Jesus.

8. My Elijah shall not compromise with Ahab and jezebel, in the name of Jesus.

9. You my Elijah, begin to raise the deed of your generation, in the name of Jesus.

10. The words and threats of Jezebel shall not scare my Elijah, in the name of Jesus.

11. Evil prophecy shall not be fulfilled in my life, in the name of Jesus.

12. You, Elisha, receive double portion, in the name of Jesus.

13. Any satanic army against my Jehoshaphat, destroy yourselves, in the name of Jesus.

14. Holy Ghost fire, burn to ashes every seed of Death upon my Destiny, in the name of Jesus.

15. Any evil sacrifice offered against my Destiny; expire, in the name of Jesus.

DAY 6

Esther 4:1, 18, 15-17

Oh Lord, Awake My Destiny

1. Every satanic army looking for my Elisha, receive blindness, in the name of Jesus.

2. Any man, woman or power, blaspheming my God, be disgraced, in the name of Jesus.

3. You, my sick Hezekiah, receive your healing, in the name of Jesus.

4. Oh Lord, take away sorrow from my table and enlarge my coasts, in the name of Jesus.

5. Any spirit of Manasseh working against my repentance, come out and die, in the name of Jesus.

6. You, my Jonah in the womb of marine spirit fish, repent and be vomited alive, in the name of Jesus.

7. You, my Daniel, jump out from the lion's cage, in the name of Jesus.

8. You, my Daniel, begin to interpret great dreams that will promote you, in the name of Jesus.

9. Oh Lord, give me a new breakthrough skill, in the name of Jesus.

10. Oh Lord, give me vision of deliverance for my generation, in the name of Jesus.

11. The evil plots of Haman against my life, backfire, in the name of Jesus.

12. My Nehemiah shall not die in captivity, my Nehemiah shall return to his possession, in the name of Jesus.

13. Every effort of Pharaoh against my life, be wasted, in the name of Jesus.

14. Oh Lord, deliver my Destiny from the demonic flood of this generation, in the name of Jesus.

15. Any evil sword, ready to smite my Destiny, smites your owner, in the name of Jesus.

DAY 7:

Esther 4:1, 8, 15-17

Oh Lord, Awake My Destiny

1. Any evil plan against my job shall fail woefully, in the name of Jesus.

2. All my Israel that has followed Absalom, be defeated in the battlefield, in the name of Jesus.

3. I refuse to look at Bath-Sheba; I will be in the battlefield, in the name of Jesus.

4. You that power that disgraced Solomon; I am not your candidate, die, in the name of Jesus.

5. You, my Enoch, you will not die in sin; begin to walk with God, in the name of Jesus.

6. Any sin that wants to destroy my Noah, be roasted by fire, in the name of Jesus.

7. You, my Abraham, leave your father's house and answer the divine call in the name of Jesus.

8. Any man, woman or power, assigned to destroy my Joseph, be disgraced, in the name of Jesus.

9. Any evil personality telling lies against my Joseph, be silenced, in the name of Jesus.

10. Oh Lord, deliver my Joseph and promote my Joseph, in the name of Jesus.

11. As a Hebrew midwife, I shall serve God instead of Pharaoh, in the name of Jesus.

12. You my Caleb, receive power to destroy the giants in the Promised Land, in the name of Jesus.

13. Every barrenness arrow fired against my Destiny, backfire, in the name of Jesus.

14. Devil, you have no option, release my Destiny by force in the name of Jesus.

15. Let the angels of the living God arise and fight for my Destiny, in the name of Jesus.

DAY 8:

Esther 4:1, 8, 15-17

Oh Lord, Awake My Destiny

1. Oh Lord, assist my Phinehas to kill the Zimris and Cozbis of my generation, in the name of Jesus.

2. Oh Lord, transform my Rehab and deliver my destiny, in the name of Jesus.

3. Any Satanic army against my Joshua, you are joking, die, die, die, in the name of Jesus.

4. You my Deborah, what are you waiting for? Begin to praise God, in the name of Jesus.

5. Any power that wants my Ruth to die in Moab, you are joking, die, in the name of Jesus.

6. Any power that wants my greatness to die in Moab, you are joking, die, in the name of Jesus.

7. Every anti-marriage spirit against my Ruth, fall down and die, in the name of Jesus.

8. Any power that wants my Abigail to marry Nabal, I reject your offer, in the name of Jesus.

9. You my David, wait until the God of vengeance kills your Saul, in the name of Jesus.

10. You the mighty men of David, destroy Absalom's people, in the name of Jesus.

11. You my Rehoboam, receive wisdom to lead your people, in the name of Jesus.

12. You my Miciah, receive boldness to prophesy, in the name of .... Jesus.

13. Satanic fish in my life, swim out and die in the name of Jesus.

14. Every Goliath of my destiny, you are finished, die in the name of Jesus.

15. Any power that wants my Destiny to be wasted, receive multiple wastage, in the name of Jesus.

16. Any power using ignorance to attack my Destiny, you are finished; die, in the name of Jesus.

17. Every cloud of impossibility surrounding my Destiny scatter by fire, in the name of Jesus.

DAY 9

Esther 4:1, 8, 15-17

Oh Lord, Awake My Destiny

1. If I am a child of God, let fire come down for my sake, in the name of Jesus.

2. The debts of my dead parents shall not terminate my life, in the name of Jesus.

3. I refuse to hand over my children to the debtors, in the name of Jesus.

4. You my Shunammite accommodate and feed Elisha of your time, in the name of Jesus.

5. My Naaman shall not die in leprosy; there is God in Israel, in the name of Jesus.

6. You my Gehazi, repent and reject leprosy, in the name of Jesus.

7. You my Jeremiah, weep for your people, in the name of Jesus.

8. You my Moses, divide your Red Sea, in the name of Jesus.

9. Oh Lord, send my Nebuchadnezzar into the bush for a lesson, in the name of Jesus.

10. My Mordeciah shall not be disgraced; he shall be promoted, in the name of Jesus.

11. You the spirit of Esther in me, what are you waiting for? Release your arrows of prayers, in the name of Jesus.

12. My elder brother shall not intimidate my David; Goliath must die, in the name of Jesus.

13. I cut the heads of my Goliath into pieces, in the name of Jesus.

14. Oh Lord, arise and multiply the fruitfulness of my Destiny, in the name of Jesus.

15. Let the cries of my Destiny receive divine visitations, in the name of Jesus.

DAY 10

Esther 4:1, 8, 15 -17

Oh Lord, Awake My Destiny

1. Oh Lord, show me my star, as in the days of the wise men from the east, in the name of Jesus.

2. You, my Joseph, you must not reject to marry; her child will save you, in the name of Jesus.

3. My publican shall sit down with Jesus, in the name of Jesus.

4. You, my Peter, begin to walk on the sea, in the name of Jesus.

5. You, the pride of the centurion, die; my centurion, beseech the Lord, in the name of Jesus.

6. Lord Jesus, touch everybody in my house as you did in the house of Peter, in the name of Jesus.

7. Lord Jesus, awake and rebuke my storm, in the name of Jesus.

8. Lord Jesus, heal all the sick in my ministry, in the name of Jesus.

9. You, my Matthew, follow Jesus immediately, in the name of   Jesus.

10. Oh Lord, allow me to anoint your feet, in the name of Jesus.

11. You my Peter, refuse to deny Christ, no matter what, in the name of Jesus.

12. Blood of Jesus, flow into my foundation and deliver my Destiny in the name of Jesus.

13. Every satanic embargo placed upon my Destiny, be lifted by force, in the name of Jesus.

14. Oh Lord, arise and spare my Destiny in the midst of mass destruction, in the name of Jesus.

15. Oh Lord, if you found my Destiny guilty, forgive him and have mercy, in the name of Jesus.

DAY 11

Esther 4:1, 8, 15-17

Oh Lord, Awake My Destiny

1. Oh Lord, heal my children as you did to the Jairus' daughter, in the name of Jesus.

2. Oh Lord, assist me to bear your cross as you did to Simon of Cyrene, in the name of Jesus.

3. Oh Lord, that answered Zechariah and Elizabeth, answer me today wherever I need your answer, in the name of Jesus.

4. Oh Lord, I am not better than the malefactor you took to heaven; remember me in your kingdom, in the name of Jesus.

5. Lord Jesus, I invite you into my life; turn my water into wine, in the name of Jesus.

6. You my Nicodemus, be broken to the glory of God, in the name of Jesus.

7.   Oh Lord, do not allow Matthias to take my position, in the name of Jesus.

8.   Oh Lord, raise a Gamaliel to talk to my Jews, in the name of Jesus.

9.   Oh Lord, help me not to use my ministry to serve tables, in the name of Jesus.

10. The enemy shall not silence my Stephen, oh Lord, open my month in wisdom, in the name of Jesus.

11. You, my Peter, begin to preach to the Gentiles, in the name of Jesus.

12. Oh Lord, bring my Barnabas and Saul together for the ministry, in the name of Jesus.

13. Oh Lord, as Paul purposed to see Rome, let me see my Rome also, in the name of Jesus.

14. Every sleeping Phebe in my ministry, arise and shine, in the name of Jesus.

15. My Destiny will not die in the strange land, in the name of Jesus.

DAY 12

Exodus 24:15-18

Oh Lord, Awake My Destiny

1. Any tree of sin against my Destiny, be uprooted by thunder, in the name of Jesus.

2. You my Adam/Eve, reject the forbidden tree completely, in the name of Jesus.

3. Any satanic Cain ready to destroy my Abel, be frustrated, in the name of Jesus.

4. Every seed of evil imagination planted inside my Destiny, die, in the name of Jesus.

5. Let the sons of Noah building evil towers against my Destiny scatter, in the name of Jesus.

6. Any programme or project without divine approval, be terminated, in the name of Jesus.

7. Any power assigned to take my Destiny to Egypt, die, in the name of Jesus.

8. I plague every Pharaoh that is ready to take another man's wife, in the name of Jesus.

9. You my herdsmen, gossiping to separate me from my helpers, die, in the name of Jesus.

10. Any Hagar despising my Sarah, leave my house by fire, in the name of Jesus.

11. Any sin of Sodom and Gomorrah attacking my Destiny, die, in the name of Jesus.

12. Any spirit of lying with determination to send me to hell, I reject you, in the name of Jesus.

13. Any deadly sickness assigned against my Destiny, catch fire in the name of Jesus.

14. Oh Lord, save my Destiny from your wrath by fire, in the name of Jesus.

15. Let the inhabitant of this city spare my Destiny by fire, in the name of Jesus.

DAY 13

Exodus 24:15-18

Oh Lord, Awake My Destiny

1. Let the seed of wickedness attacking my Destiny die, in the name of Jesus.

2. You the fire of Nadab an Abihu, you shall not burn me, in the name of Jesus.

3. Any spirit of lust, taking my mind back to Egypt, die, in the name of Jesus.

4. Every congregation of murmurers against my Destiny, scatter, in the name of Jesus.

5. You my Uzziah, remove your hand from my David, come out and die, in the name of Jesus.

6. Despise inside my heart against my David, come out and die, in the name of Jesus.

7.   You the spirit of Jebezal living inside me, manifest and die in the name of Jesus.

8.   Every spirit of falsehood in my life, die, in the name of Jesus.

9.   Any power that wants my Jeremiah to die in prison, release me and die, in the name of Jesus.

10.   You the wall of Jericho blocking my Destiny, collapse, in the name of Jesus.

11.   Spirit of disobedience, leave my Destiny alone, in the name of Jesus.

12.   Every ungodly character in my life, awaiting my Destiny, depart now, in the name of Jesus.

13.   Every enemy of my greatness, be exposed and be disgraced in the name of Jesus.

14.   Oh Lord, arise and let my Destiny resurrect by force in the name of Jesus.

15.   Anointing to rise above all the enemies of my Destiny, fall upon me in the name of Jesus.

DAY 14

Exodus 24:15-18

Oh Lord, Awake My Destiny

1.   Any spirit of the Pharisees that refuses to leave me, I force you out, in the name of Jesus.

2.   Anointing of Judas Iscariot, influencing my decision, fall down and die, in the name of Jesus.

3.   Any evil king or judge, sitting like Pilate to judge me, die, in the name of Jesus.

4.   Any tree growing in my life having only leaves without good fruit, dry up, in the name of Jesus.

5.   You the Zacharias in my life, doubting the promise of God, receive dumbness, in the name of Jesus.

6.   Any spirit of Ananias and Sapphira, ready to send me to the grave, release me by force, in the name of Jesus.

7. Elymas the sorcerer, leave your deputy alone, in the name of Jesus.

8. You the Greek inside me seeking only worldly wisdom, come out and die, in the name of Jesus.

9. You spirit of division in my Corinthians, die by fire, in the name of Jesus.

10. All ye false brethren that want to mislead my Destiny, die, in the name of Jesus.

11. Any anti-Christ spirit, eating up my Destiny, vomit it and die, in the name of Jesus.

12. Any false apostle, attacking my Destiny, kill yourself, in the name of Jesus.

13. Father Lord, defend my Destiny before his evil determined Abimelech, in the name of Jesus.

14. The inhabitant of Sodom and Gomorrah will not corrupt my Destiny, in the name of Jesus.

15. Oh Lord, open the eyes of my Destiny to see the source of prosperity, in the name of Jesus.

DAY 15

Exodus 24:15-18

Oh Lord, Awake My Destiny

1. Every enemy of the cross befriending my Destiny, be disgraced, in the name of Jesus.

2. You spirit of Hymenia's and Philetus assigned to mislead me die, in the name of Jesus.

3. Demas, Demas, Demas, leave my Destiny alone, in the name of Jesus.

4. You Alexander the coppersmith standing against my Paul, the Lord rebuke you, in the name of Jesus.

5. You my evil tongue, receive the fire of holiness, in the name of Jesus.

6. Let the spirit of the scoffers against my Destiny die, in the name of Jesus.

7. Let the power of the false doctrine assigned to destroy me die in the name of Jesus.

8. Any evil Diotrephes leading my Destiny astray, die to my favor, in the name of Jesus.

9. Let the battle between me and my Cain end to my favor, in the name of Jesus.

10. Oh Lord that destroyed Sodom and Gomorrah, destroy my Sodom and Gomorrah, in the name of Jesus.

11. You my Jacob, prevail over your angel in the name of Jesus.

12. You, my Ai, scatter, scatter, scatter in the name of Jesus.

13. You the woman of Theebez, cast your death stone against my Abimelech in the name of Jesus.

14. Let the strange fire into my bones be quenched by force in the name of Jesus.

15. Let the crying voice of my Destiny enter into the ears of my God, in the name of Jesus.

DAY 16

Exodus 24:15-18

Oh Lord, Awake My Destiny

1. You my carnal Samson, receive spiritual strength, in the name of Jesus.

2. All ye allied kings against my Israel, be defeated, in the name of Jesus.

3. You the Babylonish kingdom against my Destiny, collapse by fire in the name of Jesus.

4. You the spirit of Medis and Persians waging war against my Daniel, die in the name of Jesus.

5. All the powers seeking the life of my Moses, die before my Moses in the name of Jesus.

6. Every first-born of my stubborn Egypt, die in the midnight in the name of Jesus.

7. Mourning men and women against my Destiny, scatter, my Destiny is alive, in the name of Jesus.

8.   Let both men and women of my Jericho; die in the name of Jesus.

9.   You, my Elimelech, Mahlon and Chilion, you will not die in Moab in the name of Jesus.

10.   Every spirit of Hophni and Phinehas, assigned to mislead my Destiny, die alone in the name of Jesus.

11.   Every Agag of my destiny, die in the name of Jesus.

12.   I shall not die like the young prophet in the name of Jesus.

13.   Blood of Jesus, speak life into my dead Destiny in the name of Jesus.

14.   Oh Lord, call my Destiny out of heaven and show him the rivers of life, in the name of Jesus.

15.   You the life of my Destiny under manipulations, receive deliverance by fire, in the name of Jesus.

DAY 17

Exodus 24:15-18

Oh Lord, Awake My Destiny

1. All you, prophets of Baal standing against my Elijah, die by your own sword in the name of Jesus.

2. My Naboth shall not be slain in the field in the name of Jesus.

3. You the mighty men of Assyria against my Destiny, die in a single night in the name of Jesus.

4. I will not die like the children of Bethlehem killed by the king in the name of Jesus.

5. You my Herod, die, die and die again in the name of Jesus.

6. I refuse to be beheaded like John the Baptist in the name of Jesus.

7.   You that power that killed Destiny the beggar in poverty, my Destiny is not your candidate, in the name of Jesus.

8.   I refuse to join the company of Judas of Galilee into destruction in the name of Jesus.

9.   You the coffin of my Destiny, bury your builder alive, in the name of Jesus.

10. Let the voice of my prayers reach the cross of God in the name of Jesus.

11. Let the plague of the Egyptians be repeated against my Pharaoh in the name of Jesus.

12. Let the accusation of Israel against my Moses promote my ministry in the name of Jesus.

13. Any serpent in the root of my Destiny, come out and die in the name of Jesus.

14. Holy Ghost fire, enter into my grave to wake my Destiny in the name of Jesus.

15. Anointing to live long and fulfill my destiny, fall upon me in the name of Jesus.

DAY 18

Exodus 24:15-18

Oh Lord, Awake My Destiny

1. All the Egyptians pursuing my Israel die, in the name of Jesus.

2. Every satanic intimidation against my widowhood, promote me, in the name of Jesus.

3. This is my seventh day, oh Lord, heal my Miriam, in the name of Jesus.

4. Every consequence of sin, I am born again, die, in the name of Jesus.

5. Let the sun of my Destiny stand still until my victory is completed, in the name of Jesus.

6. Let the moon of my destiny be stayed until I win the war, in the name of Jesus.

7. Oh Lord, revive my Samson for war, in the name of Jesus.

8. Any spirit of king Saul on the throne of my life, die, in the name of Jesus.

9. Every secret plan of Saul against my David, be exposed, in the name of Jesus.

10. Let the counsel of Ahitophel against my David be rejected, in the name of Jesus.

11. My children shall not go into captivity, in the name of Jesus.

12. Any death decree against my Israel, be reversed, in the name of Jesus.

13. Let the stubborn enemy of my Lazaraus be disgraced, in the name of Jesus.

14. Oh Lord, open the eyes of my Destiny to see the invisible blessings around him, in the name of Jesus.

15. Every Rebekah of my Destiny, begin to conceive by fire, in the name of Jesus.

DAY 19

Exodus 24:15-18

Oh Lord, Awake My Destiny

1. Oh Lord, give me the divine timetable of my destiny, in the name of Jesus.

2. You my Saul of Tarsus on the way to Damascus, be arrested, in the name of Jesus.

3. You the Abraham of my destiny, take away Hagar from Sarah, in the name of Jesus.

4. Any power in Laban's house keeping my Jacob in bondage, die, in the name of Jesus.

5. You the magicians of Egypt, assigned to compete with God, be disgraced, in the name of Jesus.

6. Let men of honest report, full of the Holy Ghost, surround my ministry, in the name of Jesus.

7. Let satanic idol set up in my heart collapse now, in the name of Jesus.

8. Uzziah, Uzziah, Uzziah, mind your business; leave the ark alone, God is watching you, in the name of Jesus.

9. You my life, do not be deceived, heaven helps those who are helpless, in the name of Jesus.

10. Evil influence on the throne of Jeroboam, I am not your candidate, in the name of Jesus.

11. My Jeremiah shall not be defeated, my Jeremiah shall prophesy, in the name of Jesus.

12. Any spirit of the scribe inside me fighting against Christ, die, in the name of Jesus.

13. Every household wickedness attacking my Destiny, be put to shame, in the name of Jesus.

14. Let all the envious philistines living with my Destiny scatter in shame in the name of Jesus.

15. Every enemy of my destiny, filling the well of my Destiny with sands, die, in the name of Jesus.

DAY 20

Exodus 24:15-18

Oh Lord, Awake My Destiny

1. You my boasting, self- confident Peter, close your mouth, in the name of Jesus.

2. Oh Lord, I depend on your grace, help me in times of trials, in the name of Jesus.

3. My Destiny, wherever you are, arise by fire, in the name of Jesus.

4. Blood of Jesus, flow into the grave of my Destiny, in the name of Jesus.

5. My Destiny, what are you doing in the grave, arise and shine, in the name of Jesus.

6. Fire of God; release my Destiny immediately, in the name of Jesus.

7. Oh Lord, speak to my Destiny and quicken my Destiny, in the name of Jesus.

8. You my blind Destiny, receive your sight, in the name of Jesus.

9. You my sick Destiny, receive your healing immediately in the name of Jesus.

10. Holy Ghost, burn to ashes every witchcraft chain holing me in bondage, in the name of Jesus.

11. Wind of life; revive my dead Destiny now, in the name of Jesus.

12. Oh Lord, put life into my Destiny and quicken me, in the name of Jesus.

13. Every helper of my Destiny, appear, in the name of Jesus.

14. Every dark room of my Destiny, receive divine light, in the name of Jesus.

15. Any evil worm assigned to eat my Destiny, die, in the name of Jesus.

DAY 21

Exodus 24:15-18

Oh Lord, Awake My Destiny

1. Every darkness in my Destiny, disappear now, in the name of Jesus.

2. Resurrection power, visit my Destiny by fire, in the name of Jesus.

3. Anointing of life, fall upon my Destiny, in the name of Jesus.

4. Every satanic arrow against my Destiny, backfire, in the name of Jesus.

5. Any household witchcraft attacking my Destiny, die in the name of Jesus

6. Any seed of poverty planted against my Destiny, die in the name of Jesus.

7. Any serpent that has swallowed my Destiny, vomit it now, in the name of Jesus.

8. Every witchcraft attack against my Destiny, be terminated, in the name of Jesus.

9. Every satanic fear programmed into my Destiny, disappear.

10. Any crocodile in the water of my Destiny, die in the name of Jesus.

11. Any Delilah assigned to destroy my Destiny, die in the name of Jesus.

12. Every voice of Goliath speaking against my Destiny, be silenced, in the name of Jesus.

13. Let my Destiny reject death and receive abundant life, in the name of Jesus.

14. Let the Esau of my Destiny be blessed more than my Jacob, in the name of Jesus.

15. Father Lord, your blessing cannot finish like Isaac, bless me above my equals, in the name of Jesus.

DAY 22

Joshua 7:6-9

Oh Lord, Awake My Destiny

1.   Let the war against my Destiny; be diverted, in the name of Jesus.

2.   Let the evil plans against my Destiny be aborted, in the name of Jesus.

3.   Let my Destiny recover from every defeat now, in the name of Jesus.

4.   Satanic gunshots against my Destiny, backfire now, in the name of Jesus.

5.   Every seed of death against my Destiny, receive fire, in the name of Jesus.

6.   Wind of fire, wind of fire, wind of fire; enter into my life, in the name of Jesus.

7. My Destiny, arise, arise, arise, arise, arise and arise forever, in the name of Jesus.

8. Ever glory of my Destiny, begin to manifest by fire, in the name of Jesus.

9. Every grave cloth of my Destiny, burn to ashes now, in the name of Jesus.

10. Every limitation placed against my Destiny, disappear in the name of Jesus.

11. My Destiny, begin to fight your enemies, in the name of Jesus.

12. You, Jezebel, that is aiming to destroy my Destiny, destroy yourself, in the name of Jesus.

13. Any evil covenant assignment to destroy my Destiny; break into pieces, in the name of Jesus.

14. Any fear inside my Destiny because of Esau, disappear now, in the name of Jesus.

15. Oh Lord, let my Destiny find grace from you to overcome my Esau, in the name of Jesus.

DAY 23

Joshua 7:6-9

Oh Lord, Awake My Destiny

1. You the nakedness of my Destiny, be covered by the glory of God, in the name of Jesus.

2. You my family Destiny, receive promotion by fire, in the name of Jesus.

3. Every enemy of Destiny, scatter immediately, in the name of Jesus.

4. You my dumb Destiny, receive your healing, in the name of Jesus.

5. You my lame Destiny, arise, walk, run and fly, in the name of Jesus.

6. You the star of my lame Destiny, escape imprisonment now, in the name of Jesus.

7. Every satanic embargo against my Destiny, be lifted in the name of Jesus.

8. You the enemies of my Destiny in the heavenlies, kill yourselves, in the name of Jesus.

9. Every satanic yoke against my Destiny, break into pieces, in the name of Jesus.

10. You my Joseph, jump out of the pit by force, in the name of Jesus.

11. Oh Lord, arise in your power and change my name for better, in the name of Jesus.

12. Any reproach attached to my Destiny; disappear in shame in the name of Jesus.

13. Every promise of God to my Destiny, begin to manifest from today, in the name of Jesus.

14. The Jacob of my Destiny will not die until he fulfills his destiny in the name of Jesus.

15. The enemy of my Destiny will not harvest my destiny, in the name of Jesus.

DAY 24

Joshua 7:6-9

Oh Lord, Awake My Destiny

1. You my rejected Destiny, be accepted forever, in the name of Jesus.

2. Deaths, death, death, refuse to kill my Destiny in the name of Jesus.

3. Evil gang ups against my Destiny, scatter, scatter, scatter, in the name of Jesus.

4. Every battle against my Destiny, come to an end, in the name of Jesus.

5. Every strange fire burning my Destiny, be quenched in the name of Jesus.

6. Every witchcraft worm eating my Destiny, die, in the name of Jesus.

7. Let the stones of my prayers kill the enemies of my Destiny, in the name of Jesus.

8. Every bondage of my Destiny, begin to break by fire, in the name of Jesus.

9. Satanic soldiers against my Destiny, slay yourselves, in the name of Jesus.

10. Altars of darkness, altars of darkness, altars of darkness, release my Destiny, in the name of Jesus.

11. Every seed of death against my Destiny, die, in the name of Jesus.

12. Every enemy of my Destiny, be exposed and disgraced, in the name of Jesus.

13. Let all visitors from the dark kingdom against my Destiny be disgraced, in the name of Jesus.

14. Every bondage of my Destiny, break to pieces, in the name of Jesus.

15. Let all confusion around my Destiny be dispersed by the Holy Ghost wind, in the name of Jesus.

DAY 25

Joshua 7:6-9

Oh Lord, Awake My Destiny

1. Any satanic bungalow keeping my Destiny in bondage, release my Destiny and collapse, in the name of Jesus.

2. I rebuke the enemies of my Destiny unto death, in the name of Jesus.

3. Oh Lord, do not allow my Destiny to die, in the name of Jesus.

4. You, my Destiny in the pocket of Satan, I remove you by fire, in the name of Jesus.

5. Any jezebel against my Elijah, die, in the name of Jesus.

6. Let the sin ready to destroy my Destiny die in the name of Jesus.

7. Any agent of Satan ready to destroy my Destiny, die in the name of Jesus.

8. Thou fire of God, begin to deliver my caged Destiny, in the name of Jesus.

9. My Destiny, come out of satanic cages, in the name of Jesus.

10. You my family prison house, release my Destiny, in the name of Jesus.

11. Anything that my past sexual partner has transferred into my Destiny, dry up by fire, in the name of Jesus.

12. Oh Lord, help my Destiny to escape every danger, in the name of Jesus.

13. Every false accuser of my Destiny, be exposed and be disgraced, in the name of Jesus.

14. Oh Lord, remove every marine spirit plague placed upon my Destiny, in the name of Jesus.

15. Every serpent of death in the land of my Destiny, die in the name of Jesus.

DAY 26

Joshua 7:6-9

Oh Lord, Awake My Destiny

1. Every destructive material, produced against my Destiny, be roasted by fire, in the name of Jesus.

2. Any power sitting upon my Destiny, be unseated by fire, in the name of Jesus.

3. Any satanic prayer warrior, praying and fasting against my Destiny, be frustrated, in the name of Jesus.

4. Any evil brain, thinking against my Destiny, scatter by thunder, in the name of Jesus.

5. Any power, searching for my Destiny, be blind by fire, in the name of Jesus.

6. Oh Lord, don't allow my Destiny to die,

7. My Destiny, what are you waiting for? Move forward, in the name of Jesus.

8. Powers of God, power of God, power of God, deliver my Destiny, in the name of Jesus.

9. You the Goliath of my problems, die immediately, in the name of Jesus.

10. Any power that has vowed to disgrace my Destiny, be disgraced by fire, in the name of Jesus.

11. Oh Lord, deliver the Destiny of my marriage, in the name of Jesus.

12. Blood of Jesus, swallow the programme of Satan against my Destiny, in the name of Jesus.

13. Every unfriendly friend of my Destiny, be exposed and be disgraced, in the name of Jesus.

14. Let all the Egyptians pursuing my Destiny scatter in shame and disgrace, in the name of Jesus.

15. Oh Lord, turn a mighty strong west wind against the enemies of my Destiny, in the name of Jesus.

DAY 27

Joshua 7:6-9

Oh Lord, Awake My Destiny

1. Baptism of fire, baptize my Destiny by fire, in the name of Jesus.

2. Oh Lord, advertise my Destiny for breakthroughs, in the name of Jesus.

3. Any satanic dream targeted against my Destiny, disappear, in the name of Jesus.

4. Every evil agreement to destroy my Destiny, scatter, in the name of Jesus.

5. Any enemy of my Destiny, you will not succeed, die, in the name of Jesus.

6. Holy Ghost fire, abort by fire every pregnancy of evil in my life, in the name of Jesus.

7. Every satanic opportunity to render useless my Destiny, be frustrated, in the name of Jesus.

8. Oh Lord, spare my Destiny from evil epidemics, in the name of Jesus.

9. Any evil brain thinking against my Destiny, be disorganized, in the name of Jesus.

10. Blood of Jesus, rebuild my scattered Destiny, in the name of Jesus.

11. Every satanic agent, surrounding my Destiny, be arrested by fire, in the name of Jesus.

12. Oh Lord, set my Destiny free from captivity, in the name of Jesus.

13. Oh Lord, increase your life into my Destiny, in the name of Jesus.

14. Let the locust of God eat up every green thing in the garden of the enemies of my Destiny, in the name of Jesus.

15. I command every Pharaoh of my Destiny to be drowned in the red sea, in the name of Jesus.

DAY 28

Joshua 7:6-9

Oh Lord, Awake My Destiny

1. I jump out from any satanic circle of sorrows, in the name of Jesus.

2. Every curse placed against my Destiny, from my family's evil altars, die, in the name of Jesus.

3. I release the strength of my Destiny, by force, in the name of Jesus.

4. Any satanic judgment against my Destiny, be reversed, in the name of Jesus.

5. Let the evil sacrifice against my Destiny expire forever, in the name of Jesus.

6. Oh Lord, strengthen my Destiny by fire, in the name of Jesus.

7. Oh Lord, make me a soldier and a fighter of evil, in the name of Jesus.

8. If my Destiny is sick, oh Lord, heal me now, in the name of Jesus.

9. Evil monitor, monitoring my Destiny, scatter, in the name of Jesus.

10. Every announcement going on against my Destiny for destruction, be silenced, in the name of Jesus.

11. You the attackers against my Destiny, attack yourself now, in the name of Jesus.

12. I break and loose my Destiny from the grip of Destiny' destroyers, in the name of Jesus.

13. Powers from the waters against my Destiny, be frustrated, in the name of Jesus.

14. Every company of Satan against my Destiny, scatter in shame, in the name of Jesus.

15. Any evil power living inside my Destiny, come out and die, in the name of Jesus.

DAY 29

Joshua7:6-9

Oh Lord, Awake My Destiny

1. Any evil personality, trading with my Destiny, release me and perish, in the name of Jesus.

2. Every evil conversion against my Destiny, die, in the name of Jesus.

3. Every donation against my Destiny, disappear, in the name of Jesus.

4. Blood of Jesus, attack the attackers of my Destiny, in the name of Jesus.

5. Lord Jesus, envelop my Destiny with the blood of Jesus, in the name of Jesus.

6. Oh Lord, arrest and detain my Destiny in your perfect will, in the name of Jesus.

7. Holy Ghost fire, burn to the ground, every disease, germ eating up my Destiny, in the name of Jesus.

8. Anointing for first-class deliverance, possess me, in the name of Jesus.

9. I render useless every evil follower of my Destiny, in the name of Jesus.

10. I reject any gift targeted against my Destiny, in the name of Jesus.

11. Any evil exchange against my Destiny, I reject you by fire, in the name of Jesus.

12. Oh Lord, revive my weak Destiny by fire, in the name of Jesus.

13. Holy Spirit, Holy Spirit, Holy Spirit, take over my Destiny, in the name of Jesus.

14. Any Egyptian of my Destiny accusing me falsely, be disgraced, in the name of Jesus.

15. Let all the Egyptian soldiers pursuing my Destiny fall down and die, in the name of Jesus.

DAY 30

Joshua 7:6-9

Oh Lord, Awake My Destiny

1. Any Pilate sitting to judge my Destiny, die, in the name of Jesus.

2. Every accuser of my Destiny, receive confusion, in the name of Jesus.

3. Every chain of poverty holding my Destiny, break, in the name of Jesus.

4. Any envious enemy, planning to cage my Destiny, be frustrated immediately, in the name of Jesus.

5. Let the eagle of my Destiny begin to fly, in the name of Jesus.

6. Oh Lord, move my Destiny out of my family altar, in the name of Jesus.

7. Every baptism of failure upon my Destiny, die in the name of Jesus.

8. Anger of the Almighty, frustrate the enemies of my Destiny

9. Every satanic arrow, fired at my Destiny, backfire, in the name of Jesus.

10. Let all evil effects upon my Destiny be wiped out by the blood of Jesus.

11. Every evil programme mapped out to destroy my Destiny, be terminated, in the name of Jesus.

12. I pull down all evil kingdoms working against my Destiny, in the name of Jesus.

13. Oh Lord, arise, and cross my Destiny in dry ground by fire, in the name of Jesus.

14. Oh Lord, provide the living water for my thirsty Destiny in the wilderness, in the name of Jesus.

15. Every Amalek in the battlefield to attack my Destiny scatter in shame, in the name of Jesus.

DAY 31

Joshua 7:6-9

Oh Lord, Awake My Destiny

1. Any evil king installed against me, be paralyzed, in the name of Jesus.

2. All satanic traffic warders diverting the good things n of my destiny, be paralyzed, in the name of Jesus.

3. Let the handwriting of the enemy against my Destiny turn against the writers, in the name of Jesus.

4. I deliver my Destiny from every worldly entanglement, in the name of Jesus.

5. I break every satanic connection in earth, water and air against my Destiny, in the name of Jesus.

6. Every bondage renovator against my destiny, be totally paralyzed, in the name of Jesus.

7. Let the strongholds of debt against my destiny be totally paralyzed, in the name of Jesus.

8. Let all evil powers militating against my Destiny be consumed by fire, in the name of Jesus.

9. Any oracle or shrine working against my Destiny, be scattered in the name of Jesus.

10. Every battle, fashioned against my Destiny, backfire, in the name of Jesus.

11. Let the heavenly soldier pour down liquid fire on all the oppressors of my Destiny, in the name of Jesus.

12. Every assigned fighter against my Destiny, I bind you, in the name of Jesus.

13. Holy Ghost, incubate my Destiny by fire, in the name of Jesus.

14. Blood of Jesus, purge my Destiny by fire, in the name of Jesus.

15. You my Destiny, I release you now from every captivity, in the name of Jesus.

DAY 32

Joshua7:6-9

Oh Lord, Awake My Destiny

1. You the pound starlings and dollars of my Destiny, locate me now, in the name of Jesus.

2. Holy Ghost fire, drive away all darkness in every area of my Destiny, in the name of Jesus.

3. You my Destiny, be separated from Satan and his kingdom, in the name of Jesus.

4. I cover my Destiny with the fire of God, in the name of Jesus.

5. Every tree of profitless hard work against my Destiny, be uprooted in the name of Jesus.

6. You my Destiny, embrace the kingdom of Jesus Christ, in the name of Jesus.

7. Holy Ghost fire, deliver my Destiny, in the name of Jesus.

8. You that particular strongman against my Destiny, be bound unto death, in the name of Jesus.

9. Oh Lord, make my Destiny a channel of blessings, in the name of Jesus.

10. Every evil, bound against my Destiny, release me and scatter, in the name of Jesus.

11. I refuse to follow any evil prescription mapped out against my Destiny, in the name of Jesus.

12. You that evil strongman against my Destiny, be bound forever and ever, in the name of Jesus.

13. You my destiny, arise and shine now, in the name of Jesus.

14. Divine favor; visit my Destiny today, in the name of Jesus.

15. Let the anointing of God fall upon my Destiny, in the name of Jesus.

DAY 33

Joshua 7:6-9

Oh Lord, Awake My Destiny

1. I destroy every evil remote-controlling power, fashioned against my Destiny in the name of Jesus.

2. You that evil design, fashioned against my Destiny, I reverse you by fire in the name of Jesus.

3. Anointing of the over comer, fall upon my Destiny, in the name of Jesus.

4. Every garment of confusion upon my Destiny, be roasted by fire, in the name of Jesus.

5. Every demonic circle against my Destiny, be broken, in the name of Jesus.

6. All evil labels and stamps upon my Destiny, be cleansed out with the blood of Jesus.

7. I release my Destiny from any inherited bondage in the name of Jesus.

8. Let my God arise and scatter all witchcraft powers controlling my Destiny in the name of Jesus.

9. Every curse of automatic, failure-mechanism, working against my Destiny, backfire in the name of Jesus.

10. With the axe of God's fire, I destroy every evil plantation in the root of my Destiny in the name of Jesus.

11. Oh Lord, breathe your life giving breathe into my Destiny in the name of Jesus.

12. Any power that wants to cast my Destiny down, fall down and die, in the name of Jesus.

13. I break and lose my Destiny from every evil arrest, in the name of Jesus.

14. Let the fire of God melt away the evil stones holding my Destiny, in the name of Jesus.

15. Any evil verdict my Destiny has inherited, I reject you by fire, in the name of Jesus.

DAY 34

Joshua 7:6-9

Oh Lord, Awake My Destiny

1. Father Lord, prepare my Destiny to get to wherever you send him, in the name of Jesus.

2. Lord Jesus, increase in my Destiny daily, in the name of Jesus.

3. Father Lord, glue my Destiny together to your perfect will, in the name of Jesus.

4. You, the Destiny of my children, arise and shine in the name of Jesus.

5. My Destiny, do not run ahead of your God in the name of Jesus.

6. My Destiny, reject every inherited poverty in the name of Jesus.

7. You prayer killer, attached to my Destiny, die in the name of Jesus.

8. My Destiny will not become history while I am yet living in the name of Jesus.

9. You the mountain of my Destiny, be turned to miracles in the name of Jesus.

10. Angels of blessings, begin to bless my Destiny in the name of Jesus.

11. My Destiny, you will not tolerate poverty in the name of Jesus.

12. Every satanic chain against the marriage of my Destiny, break in the name of Jesus.

13. You my Destiny, reject the counsel of evil people in the name of Jesus.

14. Blood of Jesus, destroy every related blood sickness upon my Destiny, in the name of Jesus.

15. Blood of Jesus, flow into the grave of my Destiny now, in the name of Jesus.

DAY 35

Joshua 7:6-9

Oh Lord, Awake My Destiny

1. You, the old age of my Destiny, be renewed in the name of Jesus.

2. Any witchcraft power that wants to harvest my Destiny, die in the name of Jesus.

3. Any Herod that wants to condemn my Destiny, fall down and die in the name of Jesus.

4. Any satanic agent that has seized my Destiny, release it by force, in the name of Jesus.

5. Any satanic hospital handling my sick Destiny, discharge me by fire, in the name of Jesus.

6. Any power hindering the progress of my Destiny, be frustrated in the name of Jesus.

7. Any curse placed upon my Destiny, die in the name of Jesus.

8. Every marine bondage placed upon my Destiny, break by fire in the name of Jesus.

9. Any demonic prayer against my Destiny, backfire in the name of Jesus.

10. Blood of Jesus, wipe out every evil mark against my Destiny in the name of Jesus.

11. My Destiny shall not make a wrong choice in the name of Jesus.

12. You the enemies of my Destiny, receive multiplied shame and disgrace in the name of Jesus.

13. Every blessing that my Destiny has ever lost, be recovered in the name of Jesus.

14. Oh Lord, empower my Destiny to see your glory by fire, in the name of Jesus.

15. I release my Destiny from the control of every evil power, in the name of Jesus.

DAY 36

Joshua 7:6-9

Oh Lord, Awake My Destiny

1.   You the caged marriage of my Destiny, be released, in the name of Jesus.

2.   Every deep-rooted problem of my Destiny die, in the name of Jesus.

3.   Every deep-rooted problem of my Destiny, be uprooted in the name of Jesus.

4.   Any evil power increasing against my Destiny, scatter in the name of Jesus.

5.   I issue a death sentence on all the Goliaths of my Destiny, in the name of Jesus.

6.   Let the sword of my David touch the blood of my enemies, in the name of Jesus.

7.   Devil, you are a liar; release my Destiny now, in the name of Jesus.

8.   Every witchcraft arrest over my Destiny, be destroyed, in the name of Jesus.

9.   All the wisdom of Satan against my Destiny, die immediately, in the name of Jesus.

10.   Every internal disorder against my Destiny, receive divine order, in the name of Jesus.

11.   Every satanic infirmity in the root of my Destiny, die, in the name of Jesus.

12.   Blood of Jesus, flush every deposit of death out of the life of my Destiny, in the name of Jesus.

13.   Any good thing in my Destiny, stolen by the enemies, be recovered, in the name of Jesus.

14.   Every satanic storm planning to overthrow my Destiny, be calmed by force, in the name of Jesus.

15.   My Destiny shall testify of God's goodness again, in the name of Jesus.

DAY 37

---

1 Samuel 1:9-10

Oh Lord, awake my Destiny

1. Every hiding place and secret place of witchcraft in my Destiny, be exposed by divine fire in the name of Jesus.

2. Any witchcraft projecting death into my Destiny, die in the name of Jesus.

3. Let divine goodness possess my Destiny in the name of Jesus.

4. Every agent or sickness working against my Destiny, die by force in the name of Jesus.

5. Fire of sudden death; leave my Destiny alone in the name of Jesus.

6. Arrows of destruction, leave my Destiny now in the name of Jesus.

7. I withdraw the strength of my Destiny from fornication or adultery in the name of Jesus.

8. I dissociate my Destiny from every inherited problem in the name of Jesus.

9. Any power creating difficulties for my Destiny, be roasted in the name of Jesus.

10. Henceforth, let no principality, power, ruler of darkness, spiritual, in the name of Jesus.

11. Wickedness in the heavenlies and local wickedness trouble my Destiny, in the name of Jesus.

12. I smash into pieces, every curse and evil covenant attached to my Destiny, in the name of Jesus.

13. Every enemy of my Destiny, be banished now, in the name of Jesus.

14. Let all satanic grips over my Destiny be released, in the name of Jesus.

15. Let the power that delivered Paul and Silas deliver my Destiny, in the name of Jesus

DAY 38

---

1 Samuel 1:9-10

Oh Lord, awake my Destiny

1. Any evil growth in my Destiny, be uprooted by fire, in the name of Jesus.

2. Blood of Jesus, mingled with Holy Ghost fire, sanitize my Destiny in the name of Jesus.

3. Any strange power attacking my Destiny, die in the name of Jesus.

4. Angels of God, brush off the love of strange women/men completely from my heart in the name of Jesus.

5. Oh Lord, create the wall of fire between failure and my Destiny, in the name of Jesus.

6. I remove my Destiny from the book of seers of goodness without manifestation, in the name of Jesus.

7. The pregnancy of good things within my Destiny will not be aborted, in the name of Jesus.

8. All demonically organized networks against my Destiny, be put to shame, in the name of Jesus.

9. Oh Lord, do not terminate your divine purpose for my Destiny, in the name of Jesus.

10. My Lord, my God, raise my Destiny from the grave by thunder, in the name of Jesus.

11. Any decision against my Destiny, backfire, in the name of Jesus.

12. Every adversity against my Destiny, receive shame, in the name of Jesus.

13. You the power that has wasted my parents Destiny, now attacking me, die, in the name of Jesus.

14. Any power that wants to use my Destiny and dump it die, in the name of Jesus.

15. I anoint my Destiny against the poison of death, in the name of Jesus.

DAY 39

---

1 Samuel 1:9-10

Oh Lord, awake my Destiny

1.   All you enemies of my Destiny, receive darkness, in the name of Jesus.

2.   Let confusion pursue all the enemies of my Destiny, in the name of Jesus.

3.   Every Haman of my Destiny, why are you alive? Die by fire, in the name of Jesus.

4.   I move my Destiny from bondage to liberty, in the name of Jesus.

5.   I cut my Destiny off completely from the oppressors, in the name of Jesus.

6.   Father Lord, remove spiritual cataract from the eyes of my Destiny, in the name of Jesus.

7.   Father Lord, open up the spiritual understanding of my Destiny, in the name of Jesus.

8.   Let the evil weakness in my Destiny receive termination by fire, in the name of Jesus.

9.   Any power hindering the greatness of my Destiny, die, in the name of Jesus

10.   All buried Destiny; begin to come forth, in the name of Jesus.

11.   Every dark work done against my Destiny, be exposed to shame, in the name of Jesus.

12.   Let unprofitable marks in my Destiny; be erased by fire, in the name of Jesus.

13.   Every arrow of death, fired against my Destiny, backfire, in the name of Jesus.

14.   Every demonic pestilence upon my Destiny disappears by force, in the name of Jesus.

15.   Every rage of the enemy against my Destiny, backfire, in the name of   Jesus.

DAY 40

---

1 Samuel 1:9-10

Oh Lord, awake my Destiny

1.   Oh Lord, assist my Destiny to overcome all obstacles to my breakthroughs in the name of Jesus.

2.   Every instrument of the enemy fashioned against my Destiny, break, into pieces, in the name of Jesus.

3.   Every evil trap set against my Destiny, catch my enemy, in the name of Jesus

4.   I remove the peace of the enemies of my Destiny, in the name of Jesus.

5.   Every conspirator of my Destiny, I break your backbone, in the name of Jesus.

6.   Devil, take your hands and legs away from the affairs of my Destiny, in the name of Jesus.

7.   I bind every strongman holding my marriage captive, in the name of Jesus.

8. Father Lord, restore all the wasted years of my Destiny, in the name of Jesus.

9. Unmerited favor, flow into my Destiny by fire, in the name of Jesus.

10. Every good thing presently eluding my Destiny, begin to flow into it, in the name of Jesus.

11. Father Lord, bring honey out of the rock for my Destiny, in the name of Jesus

12. Finance shall no longer embarrass my Destiny, in the name of Jesus.

13. Axe of God, break the backbone of the enemies of my Destiny, in the name of Jesus.

14. Oh Lord, send your angel to bring me out of the Egyptian bondages, in the name of Jesus.

15. Every satanic pit waiting to swallow my Destiny, close, in the name of Jesus.

DAY 41

---

1 Kings 19:1-8

Oh Lord, awake my Destiny

1. You, the destroyer of my Destiny, be destroyed, in the name of Jesus.

2. You the power of the oppressor troubling my Destiny, destroy yourselves, in the name of Jesus.

3. I receive victory over all the forces fighting against my Destiny, in the name of Jesus.

4. I stand victorious over all the forces fighting against my Destiny, in the name of Jesus

5. Anointing of poverty harassing my Destiny, break, in the name of Jesus.

6. Anointing of barrenness and miscarriage insulting my marriage, die by fire in the name of Jesus.

7. Anointing of late marriage against my Destiny, break into pieces, in the name of Jesus.

8. Oh Lord, give me a miracle that will comfort my Destiny, in the name of Jesus.

9. The God who delivered the children of Israel from Pharaoh, deliver my Destiny, in the name of Jesus.

10. The power that dealt with Sodom and Gomorrah, deal with the enemies of my Destiny, in the name of Jesus.

11. Oh God, arise and fight for my Destiny, in the name of Jesus.

12. Thou God that sent Nebuchadnezzar into the wilderness, repeat your work against my Nebuchadnezzar, in the name of Jesus.

13. Any serpent biting my Destiny, bite your sender and die, in the name of Jesus.

14. Let the fiery serpent come out and bite the enemies of my Destiny unto death, in the name of Jesus.

15. Every evil vessel, fashioned against my Destiny, be roasted, in the name of Jesus.

DAY 42

---

1 Kings 19:1-8

Oh Lord, awake my Destiny

1. Father Lord, answer my prayers the same way you answered Elijah, in the name of Jesus.

2. Let the fire of God fall upon my Destiny, in the name of Jesus.

3. Grave, grave, grave, open and release my Destiny, in the name of Jesus.

4. That voice that delivered the dead Destiny, speak to my Destiny, in the name of Jesus.

5. Let there be destruction in the camp of the enemies of my Destiny, in the name of Jesus

6. My Destiny must fulfill its divine destiny, in the name of Jesus.

7. I receive the mandate to put to flight every enemy of my Destiny, in the name of Jesus.

8. Oh Lord, restore all the lost testimonies of my Destiny, in the name of Jesus.

9. Let the fire and thunder of God destroy every demonic padlock holding my Destiny, in the name of Jesus.

10. Every demonic eye, monitoring my Destiny, be blinded, in the name of Jesus

11. Every inner voice speaking against my Destiny, be silenced, in the name of Jesus.

12. I claim every divine promise concerning my Destiny, in the name of Jesus.

13. Father Lord, lift my Destiny up above all my enemies, in the name of Jesus.

14. Every inheritance of my Destiny, begin to manifest by fire, in the name of Jesus.

15. Any witchcraft pot, cooking my Destiny, breaking into pieces, in the name of Jesus.

DAY 43

---

1 Kings 19:1-8

Oh Lord, awake my Destiny

1. Any unfriendly friend, confusing my Destiny, receive confusion, in the name of Jesus.

2. Every extra-marital relationship, fashioned to destroy my Destiny, die prematurely, in the name of Jesus.

3. All boasting powers, speaking against my Destiny, be silenced, in the name of Jesus.

4. Every benefit of my Destiny in the hands of my oppressors, I take you by force in the name of Jesus.

5. Any power chasing away the blessing of my Destiny, die immediately, in the name of Jesus.

6. You the blessings of my Destiny eaten up by the enemy, be vomited, in the name of Jesus.

7.   Oh Lord, ignite the prayer power of my Destiny, in the name of Jesus.

8.   My Destiny shall not operate below divine expectation, in the name of Jesus.

9.   Father Lord, clear spiritual clogs from my Destiny, in the name of Jesus.

10.   Let the strength of the strongman against my Destiny be taken by force, in the name of Jesus.

11.   My Destiny must rejoice over her enemies at the end of this programme, in the name of Jesus.

12.   You the spirit of resistance and carry-overs, my Destiny, is not your candidate, in the name of Jesus.

13.   Any evil power cooking the destiny of my Destiny, be Frustrated, in the name of Jesus.

14.   Any witchcraft attack against my Destiny, be terminated, in the name of Jesus.

15.   I refuse to lock out my Destiny from blessings, in the name of Jesus.

DAY 44

---

1 Kings 19:1-8

Oh Lord, awake my Destiny

1. My Destiny, reject all evil habitations, in the name of Jesus.

2. You evil foreign hands, laid on my Destiny, dry up, in the name of Jesus.

3. Any local power determined against my Destiny, die by force, in the name of Jesus.

4. Let creative miracles visit the grave of my Destiny now, in the name of Jesus.

5. All spirits rooted in immorality against my Destiny, come out with all your roots, in the name of Jesus.

6. Every arrow of fear, fired at my Destiny, die, in the name of Jesus.

7. You the spirit wife/husband against my Destiny, die, in the name of Jesus.

8. Every information about my Destiny is lost to the marine powers, in the name of Jesus.

9. Let the true fire of God enter into my Destiny now, in the name of Jesus.

10. I receive complete deliverance meant for my Destiny, in the name of Jesus.

11. Every affected evil part of my Destiny, be healed, in the name of Jesus.

12. Oh Lord, separate my Destiny from the spirit of death, in the name of Jesus.

13. Every rebellion against my   Destiny, be scattered by thunder, in the name of Jesus.

14. Any foundational problem standing against my Destiny to Canaan, die, in the name of Jesus.

15. Every satanic identification mark against my Destiny, be wiped out by the blood of Jesus, in the name of Jesus.

DAY 45

---

1 Kings 19:1-8

Oh Lord, awake my Destiny

1. Oh Lord, bring my Destiny into favor before great men, in the name of Jesus.

2. Every demonic delay, targeted at my Destiny, be removed, in the name of Jesus.

3. I destroy every spirit of antagonism against my Destiny, in the name of Jesus.

4. Let the evil collaborators against my Destiny scatter, in the name of Jesus.

5. Every demonic opinion against my destiny, I bind and render you to naught, in the name of Jesus.

6. Every evil manipulation fashioned against my Destiny, I reject you now, in the name of Jesus.

7. Blood of Jesus, reverse all evil covenant and curses against my Destiny, in the name of Jesus.

8.   Let God arise in His anger and defend my Destiny, in the name of Jesus.

9.   Any attack against my Destiny from my past sinful life, be terminated, in the name of Jesus.

10.   Every Destiny destroyer in my life, I come against you, in the name of Jesus.

11.   Oh Lord, smite every evil tongue rising up against you, in the name of Jesus.

12.   I convert my Destiny into untouchable coals of fire, in the name of Jesus.

13.   Oh Lord, uproot everything you have not planted in my Destiny, in the name of Jesus.

14.   Father Lord, give my Destiny the programme sheet of his destiny, in the name of Jesus.

15.   Every troublesome arrow, fired at my Destiny, backfire, in the name of Jesus.

DAY 46

---

1 Kings 19:1-8

Oh Lord, awake my Destiny

1. Every wicked meeting being held against my Destiny, be disbanded, in the name of Jesus.

2. Every curse of impossibility issued against my Destiny, backfire, in the name of Jesus.

3. Oh Lord, help me to recover my Destiny, in the name of Jesus.

4. I disconnect my Destiny from the evil family river, in the name of Jesus.

5. Every spiritual vulture on my destiny, die by fire, in the name of Jesus.

6. Every satanic decree against my Destiny, be revoked, in the name of Jesus.

7. Every evil utterance against my Destiny, be silenced, in the name of Jesus.

8. All evil powers sitting on my promotion, be unseated, in the name of Jesus.

9. Any spirit of foolishness attached to my Destiny, be detached by fire, in the name of Jesus.

10. My Destiny shall not be misplaced, in the name of Jesus.

11. Father, in the name of Jesus, spare my Destiny from destruction, in the name of Jesus.

12. Every agent of shame working against my Destiny, be paralyzed, in the name of Jesus.

13. Any chain of death dragging my Destiny, break, in the name of Jesus.

14. Every stronghold, attacking my Destiny, be dismantled, in the name of Jesus.

15. Every misguiding power, tossing my Destiny about, die, in the name of Jesus.

DAY 47

---

1 Kings 19:1-8

Oh Lord, awake my Destiny

1. Oh Lord, fill my Destiny with wisdom, in the name of Jesus.

2. You, my Destiny, receive divine direction, in the name of Jesus.

3. Every strong voice of iniquity assigned to speak against my lazars, be silenced, in the name of Jesus.

4. Powers of darkness assigned against my Destiny, scatter, in the name of Jesus.

5. I stand against the satanic re-arrangement of my destiny, in the name of Jesus.

6. Oh Lord, enlarge the coast of my Destiny, in the name of Jesus.

7. All evil powers, caring negative awareness of my Destiny, be impotent in the name of Jesus.

8. Every evil observer of my Destiny, be paralyzed in the name of Jesus.

9. All witchcraft handwritings against my destiny, be wiped by the blood of Jesus in the name of Jesus.

10. Every evil bullet targeted against my business, backfire in the name of Jesus.

11. You spirit of death and hell ready to destroy my destiny, be diverted in the name of Jesus.

12. Every iron-like curse against my marriage, be cancelled, in the name of Jesus.

13. Any evil foundation power attacking my Destiny, drink the blood of Jesus, in the name of Jesus.

14. Any satanic farmer, planting in my foundation, die, in the name of Jesus.

15. You, the demonic attack against my Destiny, die, in the name of Jesus.

DAY 48

1 Kings 19:1-8

Oh Lord, awake my Destiny

1. Any strange money in my business, I remove you by force, in the name of Jesus.

2. Every star hijacker, ready to hijack my Destiny, die by fire, in the name of Jesus.

3. You, the strong enemy of my Destiny, receive the rain of affliction, in the name of Jesus.

4. Let the multiple evil covenants attacking my Destiny be broken by fire, in the name of Jesus.

5. All counterfeit blessings following my Destiny, disappear, in the name of Jesus.

6. Every desert spirit, pursuing my Destiny, die, in the name of Jesus.

7. All ye evil reporter, assigned against my Destiny, be overthrown, in the name of Jesus.

8. Every spirit of tragedy against my Destiny, disappear forever, in the name of Jesus.

9. You the powers that arrest progress, I am not your candidate, in the name of Jesus.

10. Every wicked broadcaster in the foundation of my life, die, in the name of Jesus.

11. Every amputator of great Destiny in my family line, collapse and die, in the name of Jesus.

12. Satanic ministers, minister death into your own kingdom, in the name of Jesus.

13. Blood of Jesus, speak deliverance unto my Destiny, in the name of Jesus.

14. Oh Lord, lead my Destiny to ask counsel before any action, in the name of Jesus.

15. You, my Destiny, rise above unbelievers around you, in the name of Jesus.

DAY 49

---

1 Kings 19:1-8

Oh Lord, Awake My Destiny

1. Any evil, searching for my Destiny, die, in the name of Jesus.

2. Demons in the rocks, assigned against my marriage, I bury you alive, in the name of Jesus.

3. You vagabond anointing upon my Destiny, disappear, in the name of Jesus

4. Every dark agent in my father's house, be exposed, in the name of Jesus.

5. Any power contending with my angels of blessings, fall down and die, in the name of Jesus.

6. Any roundabout spirit limiting my Destiny, die, in the name of Jesus.

7. Every coffin spirit, targeting my Destiny, be destroyed, in the name of Jesus.

8.   Every garment of darkness upon my Destiny, be roasted, in the name of Jesus.

9.   Any evil planted in my Destiny by the enemy, come out and die, in the name of Jesus.

10.   The rod of the wicked shall not rest upon my Destiny, in the name of Jesus.

11.   Every internal warfare in my destiny, be quenched, in the name of Jesus.

12.   Any local chain tormenting my Destiny, die, in the name of Jesus.

13.   Any power, assigned to corrupt my labor die, in the name of Jesus

14.   I shake out every serpent attached to my Destiny, in the name of Jesus.

15.   Father Lord, give my Destiny a life-changing success by fire, in the name of Jesus.

DAY 50

---

1 Kings 19:1-8

Oh Lord, awake my Destiny

1. Every satanic opportunity against my Destiny, I take you away, in the name of Jesus.

2. You satanic night raiders, I destroy your weapons, in the name of Jesus.

3. I remove the food and drinks of my stubborn enemies, in the name of Jesus.

4. Every internal thief on my destiny, die by fire, in the name of Jesus.

5. No evil family river shall flow into my Destiny, in the name of Jesus.

6. I withdraw my Destiny from ungodly friendships, in the name of Jesus.

7. I destroy every evil influence against my Destiny by fire, in the name of Jesus.

8. Holy Ghost fire, possess my Destiny by fire, in the name of Jesus.

9. My Destiny shall not come to the world in vain, in the name of Jesus.

10. I reject every satanic re-arrangement of my Destiny, in the name of Jesus.

11. Every evil effort to change my destiny, I resist your powers unto death, in the name of Jesus.

12. Any agent of Satan polluting my Destiny, die, in the name of Jesus.

13. Evil arrows that refused to let my Destiny go, catch fire, in the name of Jesus.

14. Let all the Midianites oppressing my Destiny be scattered unto death, in the name of Jesus.

15. Holy Ghost power, project my Destiny to prosperity, in the name of Jesus.

DAY 51

---

2 Chronicles 20:1-3, 22, 23

Oh Lord, Awake My Destiny

1. Any power contending with my Destiny, die, in the name of Jesus.

2. My Destiny will not give up; my Destiny shall win the battle, in the name of Jesus.

3. My Destiny shall not accept any defeat, in the name of Jesus.

4. Satan shall not regulate my progress, in the name of Jesus.

5. Every bird of death against my Destiny, die, in the name of Jesus.

6. My Destiny shall not suffer confusion, in the name of Jesus.

7. Any satanic worm in the blood of my Destiny, die, in the name of Jesus.

8.   I fire back, every occultic arrow fired at my Destiny, in the name of Jesus.

9.   Any power of witchcraft, bewitching my business, be frustrated, in the name of Jesus.

10. Every satanic reinforcement against my Destiny, be exposed to shame, in the name of Jesus.

11. Every hidden oppressor against my Destiny, be exposed to shame, in the name of Jesus.

12. Evil arrester assigned to arrest my Destiny, be arrested, in the name of Jesus.

13. Oh Lord, arise and let the story of my Destiny change, in the name of Jesus.

14. Oh Lord, revive my dead Destiny by your power, in the name of Jesus.

15. Every stronghold of marine witchcraft, built against my Destiny, collapse, in the name of Jesus.

DAY 52

---

2 Corinthians 20:1-3, 22, 23

Oh Lord, Awake My Destiny

1. You, my Destiny' personalized strongholds, collapse by thunder, in the name of Jesus.

2. You my wandering star, go to your place, in the name of Jesus.

3. Any evil traffic warden stopping my Destiny, fall down and die, in the name of Jesus.

4. Every gate of evil against my destiny, be uprooted, in the name of Jesus.

5. Any dream manipulator, manipulating my Destiny in the dream, die, in the name of Jesus.

6. I fire back, every arrow of fruitless effort against my labors, in the name of Jesus.

7. Any seed of marriage killer living inside me, come out and die, in the name of Jesus.

8. Every seed of late progress, planted in my life, die, in the name of Jesus.

9. You distributors of shame, I am not your candidate, in the name of Jesus.

10. Any power caging my Destiny, you are wicked; therefore, die, in the name of Jesus.

11. Any evil transfer, working against my Destiny, be frustrated, in the name of Jesus.

12. You, my twin brother/sister attacking my Destiny, die, in the name of Jesus.

13. Holy Ghost fire, burn into ashes the wall of Jericho of my Destiny, in the name of Jesus.

14. By the power in the blood of Jesus, let my Destiny arise, in the name of Jesus.

15. Oh Lord, deliver my Destiny from the curses of witchcrafts, in the name of Jesus.

DAY 53

---

2 Chronicles 20:1-3, 22, 23

Oh Lord, Awake My Destiny

1. Divine whirlwind, take my Destiny away from shame, in the name of Jesus.

2. Destroying flood of God, destroy all evil altars in my place of birth, in the name of Jesus.

3. Oh Lord, send raging fire against my infirmities, in the name of Jesus.

4. Let the brain of my Pharaoh receive madness, in the name of Jesus.

5. Witchcraft powers against my marriage, receive unbearable heat unto death, in the name of Jesus.

6. Cloud of sorrow, possess the enemies of my Destiny, in the name of Jesus

7. Divine confusion; take over every evil brain thinking against my Destiny, in the name of Jesus.

8. Witches and wizards in this area, networking against my Destiny, receive double disappointment, in the name of Jesus.

9. Let my Destiny escape every witchcraft exposition, in the name of Jesus.

10. My stubborn Goliath, receive bitter destruction, in the name of Jesus.

11. Great furnace, meet my enemies in their bedroom, in the name of Jesus.

12. Every evil priest, preparing harm against my Destiny, eat the bread of affliction, in the name of Jesus.

13. Every garment of poverty upon my Destiny, catch fire, in the name of Jesus.

14. Every stone of shame about to touch my Destiny, backfire, in the name of Jesus.

15. I send the divine fire of judgment to the camp of my enemies, in the name of Jesus.

DAY 54

---

2 Corinthians 20:1-3, 22, 23

Oh Lord, Awake My Destiny

1. Every determined evil priest working day and night to kill my Destiny, kill your consultants and die, in the name of Jesus.

2. Any evil eye, monitoring my destiny from my place of birth, receive blindness in the name of Jesus.

3. Fire of day and night; follow my Herod to the graveyard, in the name of Jesus.

4. Every stubborn curse against my destiny, break into pieces, in the name of Jesus.

5. Every stubborn curse against my destiny, be broken, in the name of Jesus.

6. I restore my sense to its original position, in the name of Jesus.

7. You my spiritual evil parents, die, die, and die, in the name of Jesus.

8. I reject every love advance of the Delilah, in the name of Jesus.

9. Anger of the Lord, kill my Haman, in the name of Jesus.

10. My Goliath, receive shock and die, in the name of Jesus.

11. I use concentrated acid against marine witchcraft, working against my Destiny, in the name of Jesus.

12. Let great earthquakes visit the evil altars attacking my Destiny, in the name of Jesus.

13. Father Lord, Deliver my Destiny from the sins of my father house, in the name of Jesus.

14. Any power that has shut the womb of my Destiny blessings, open it by force, in the name of Jesus.

15. I release my womb from every curse of corruption of the reproductive organs, in the name of Jesus.

DAY 55

---

2 Corinthians 20:1-3, 22, 23

Oh Lord, Awake My Destiny

1. Let there be a seaquake in the rivers of my destiny, in the name of Jesus.

2. I send horrible tempests against every marine agent on assignment to destroy me, in the name of Jesus.

3. I take away from my body, every piece of spiritual grave cloth against my destiny, in the name of Jesus.

4. Every unprofitable, evil load upon my life, fall off now, in the name of Jesus.

5. Any evil advertisement, going on against my Destiny, be silenced, in the name of Jesus.

6. My Destiny, I move you to divine traffic lights, in the name of Jesus.

7. I cut my Destiny free from the hands of serpents and scorpions, in the name of Jesus.

8. Every evil kingdom, raging against my Destiny, scatter by thunder, in the name of Jesus.

9. Any power that wants to suffocate my Destiny, be suffocated, in the name of Jesus.

10. Any personality, hiding the keys of my elevation, release it and die, in the name of Jesus.

11. Any evil power, hunting my Destiny, die, in the name of Jesus.

12. Any power, sitting on an evil mat against my Destiny, fall down and die, in the name of Jesus.

13. I command my Destiny to be available for all manners of miracles, in the name of Jesus.

14. You my Destiny arise and cry for a change, in the name of Jesus.

15. Though hands join with hands, all the enemies of my Destiny shall be punished, in the name of Jesus.

DAY 56

---

2 Corinthians 20:1-3, 22, 23

Oh Lord, Awake My Destiny

1. Oh Lord, cause my proposals to be hot for the enemy to sit upon, in the name of Jesus.

2. I transfer the riches of the Gentiles into my accounts, in the name of Jesus.

3. All my confiscated blessings, I recover you now, in the name of Jesus.

4. Every ordination of lateness to my breakthrough, I shake you off, in the name of Jesus.

5. I wash away every reproach by the blood of Jesus Christ, in the name of Jesus.

6. Prince of Persia blocking my way, fall down and die, in the name of Jesus.

7. Oh Lord, make a way of easy success for me, in the name of Jesus.

8.   I plead the blood of Jesus over my Destiny, in the name of Jesus.

9.   Every strange mark on my life, be rubbed off by the precious blood of Jesus Christ, in the name of Jesus.

10. Every evil vow, made by my parents upon my life, break now, in the name of Jesus.

11. I withdraw my Destiny from every evil group, be removed now, in the name of Jesus.

12. Every habit of my parent, attacking my Destiny, I reject you by fire, in the name of Jesus.

13. Any evil occurrence against my Destiny from my father's house disappear, in the name of Jesus.

14. Every serpent in the foundation of my Destiny, die, in the name of Jesus.

DAY 57

---

2 Corinthians 20:1-3, 22, 23

Oh Lord, Awake My Destiny

1. My Destiny, stop repeating the mistakes of my parents, in the name of Jesus.

2. Thou king of kings, deliver my Destiny from destruction, in the name of Jesus.

3. My Destiny, receive fire by fire, in the name of Jesus.

4. Whatsoever is bewitching my Destiny, I bind such powers, in the name of Jesus.

5. I shall not speak against my Destiny, in the name of Jesus.

6. Holy Ghost fire, purge my Destiny by fire, in the name of Jesus.

7. You my tongue, receive divine power to favor my, Destiny in the name of Jesus

8. Every devourer against my handiwork, die, in the name of Jesus.

9. Any imperfection in my destiny, die by force, in the name of Jesus.

10. Oh Lord, arise and command deliverance upon my Destiny, in the name of Jesus.

11. Blood of Jesus, heal my business by fire, in the name of Jesus.

12. Every satanic battle confronting my Destiny, die by thunder, in the name of Jesus.

13. Let the ancestral strongman pursuing my Destiny be disgraced, in the name of Jesus.

14. Oh Lord, speak your word of life unto my dead Destiny, in the name of Jesus.

DAY 58

---

2 Corinthians 20:1-3, 22, 23

Oh Lord, Awake My Destiny

1. Every spirit of wrong investment, attacking my decision, I reject you, in the name of Jesus.

2. Eternal Rock of Ages, roll away the stones of death upon my Destiny, in the name of Jesus.

3. Father Lord, have mercy upon my soul and revive my Destiny, in the name of Jesus.

4. Oh Lord, advertise your mercy upon my life, in the name of Jesus.

5. Father Lord, saturate my Destiny with your fire of glory, in the name of Jesus.

6. Let the arrows of sorrow flying against my Destiny locate my Haman, in the name of Jesus.

7. Lord, deliver my Destiny from impurity, in the name of Jesus.

8.   This year shall not bury my Destiny, in the name of Jesus.

9.   Every satanic temple against my Destiny, be uprooted by thunder, in the name of Jesus.

10.   Let signs and wonders possess my Destiny, in the name of Jesus.

11.   Oh Lord, let my Destiny reach its promised land, in the name of Jesus.

12.   Every enemy of my Destiny shall bow, in the name of Jesus.

13.   Every evil sacrifice against my Destiny, expire, in the name of Jesus

14.   Powers that kill and bury, my Destiny is not your candidate, in the name of Jesus.

DAY 59

---

2 Corinthians 20:1-3, 22, 23

Oh Lord, Awake My Destiny

1. You, my Destiny, receive promotion by fire, in the name of Jesus.

2. Every satanic verdict against my Destiny, be reversed, in the name of Jesus.

3. Every satanic desire against my Destiny, be frustrated, in the name of Jesus

4. Evil diviners against my Destiny, receive confusion, in the name of Jesus.

5. Let satanic darkness covering my glory disappear, in the name of Jesus.

6. I use the blood of Jesus against every enemy of my Destiny, in the name of Jesus.

7. Every gate of brass blocking my Destiny, open by force, in the name of Jesus.

8. You my imprisoned Destiny, leave the prison yard now, in the name of Jesus.

9. Divine power from heaven; deliver my Destiny, in the name of Jesus.

10. Great arm of the Lord of the Lords, break every bondage of my Destiny, in the name of Jesus.

11. You my stolen blessings, begin to come back now, in the name of Jesus.

12. In any way my Destiny is held captive, oh Lord, release it now, in the name of Jesus.

13. Spirit of sickness and disease, planted into my Destiny, come out and die, in the name of Jesus.

14. Father Lord, arise, fight and deliver my Destiny, in the name of Jesus.

DAY 60

---

2 Corinthians 20:1-3, 22, 23

Oh Lord, Awake My Destiny

1. Whoever has vowed to kill my Destiny shall fail, in the name of Jesus.

2. Thou arm of God, arise and fight for my Destiny, in the name of Jesus.

3. Let the voice of divine judgment destroy the enemy of my destiny, in the name of Jesus.

4. Peace of God, possess my Destiny by fire, in the name of Jesus.

5. Holy Ghost fire, it is time for my Destiny to arise, begin to manifest, in the name of Jesus.

6. You the power raising evil dreams against my life, die, in the name of Jesus.

7. Evil government of my father's house, collapse, in the name of Jesus.

8. Every evidence of failure upon my Destiny, disappear, in the name of Jesus.

9. Any evil priest, manipulating my destiny, be frustrated, in the name of Jesus.

10. You, the contrary power aborting good things out of my life, die, in the name of Jesus.

11. Every sexual act against my life, perish, in the name of Jesus.

12. You, the power that vowed to kill my Destiny, kill your sender, in the name of Jesus.

13. Any evil veil covering the glory of my Destiny, burn into ashes, in the name of Jesus.

14. You my Destiny, arise and possess your possessions, in the name of Jesus.

DAY 61

Joel 2:12-17

Oh Lord, Awake My Destiny

1. Let the strange voice giving my destiny strange commands in dreams die, in the name of Jesus.

2. All my glory, taken away by household wickedness, be restored by fire, in the name of Jesus.

3. God of Elijah, deliver my Destiny from witchcraft, in the name of Jesus.

4. You my Destiny, be protected from witchcraft attacks, in the name of Jesus.

5. Any evil pattern in my marriage, die, in the name of Jesus.

6. Every shame attached to my Destiny, disappear, in the name of Jesus.

7. I approach the graveyard of my Destiny; disappear, in the name of Jesus.

8. Covenant of death, inherited from my ancestors; die, in the name of Jesus.

9. Every mark of hatred upon my Destiny, be wiped by the blood of Jesus, in the name of Jesus.

10. Any evil summons against my Destiny, backfire, in the name of Jesus.

11. You my Destiny in captivity, disappear, in the name of Jesus.

12. Every kind of shame following my Destiny about, die, in the name of Jesus.

13. I command all evil commandments against my Destiny, to backfire, in the name of Jesus.

14. Every weapon fashioned against my Destiny, you are finished die, in the name of Jesus.

DAY 62

Joel 2:12-17

Oh Lord, Awake My Destiny

1. Let the arrows of sickness shot at my Destiny backfire, in the name of Jesus.

2. Let the glory which sexual sin has taken from me be restored, in the name of Jesus.

3. Any evil giant, looking for how to destroy my Destiny shall die, in the name of Jesus.

4. I receive the anointing to possess my possession, in the name of Jesus.

5. Every embargo upon my Destiny, be lifted, in the name of Jesus.

6. Every satanic battle in my life, end, in the name of Jesus.

7. Any evil personality, using the sun, moon and stars against my Destiny, fail woefully, in the name of Jesus.

8. All evil meetings organized against my glory, scatter in the name of Jesus.

9. Any power, attacking my Destiny, I confront you by fire in the name of Jesus.

10. Let the evil forces from my father's house destroy themselves, in the name of Jesus.

11. Any power from the waters, eating up the glories of my Destiny, be unseated, in the name of Jesus.

12. Whatsoever must happen for my Destiny to come first, let it happen now, in the name of Jesus.

13. Blood of Jesus, convert every evil speech against my Destiny, into favor, in the name of Jesus.

14. I command my Destiny to arise and move forward, in the name of Jesus.

DAY 63

Joel 2:12-17

Oh Lord, Awake My Destiny

1. My Destiny, flee from every danger and destruction, in the name of Jesus.

2. Any wicked personality, working against my marriage, die, in the name of Jesus.

3. Evil battle and evil altars together against my Destiny, be disgraced, in the name of Jesus.

4. I close by death every mouth of Goliath opened against my Destiny, in the name of Jesus.

5. Any power increasing my sorrow, be disappointed, in the name of Jesus.

6. Thou house of evil, my Destiny is not your candidate, in the name of Jesus.

7. Let the flood of ungodly men planning against my Destiny scatter, in the name of Jesus.

8. Every stronghold against my Destiny, collapse, in the name of Jesus.

9. Spirit of divine success, possess my Destiny, in the name of Jesus.

10. Every spy of darkness against my destiny, receive blindness, in the name of Jesus.

11. Every spirit of backwardness against my Destiny, die, in the name of Jesus.

12. Let the vagabond anointing disappear from my destiny, in the name of Jesus.

13. I separate my Destiny from every demonic captivity, in the name of Jesus.

14. Oh Lord, take away my Destiny from among the dead, in the name of Jesus.

DAY 64

Joel 2:12-17

Oh Lord, Awake My Destiny

1. Every late progress anointing upon my destiny, I remove you by fire, in the name of Jesus.

2. Let the spirit of the graveyard flee from my Destiny in the name of Jesus.

3. My Destiny, wake up and possess your possession, in the name of Jesus.

4. Every spirit of stagnancy, leave my Destiny alone, in the name of Jesus.

5. You my Destiny, drink the waters of life, in the name of Jesus.

6. Let irreversible success come upon my Destiny, in the name of Jesus

7. Divine light; remove the darkness in my destiny, in the name of Jesus.

8. Power of resurrection, quicken my Destiny, in the name of Jesus.

9. Great God, promote my Destiny by fire, in the name of Jesus.

10. Divine presence; swallow my Destiny, in the name of Jesus.

11. Blessed Holy Trinity, show yourself in my Destiny, in the name of Jesus.

12. You, the coast of my Destiny, be enlarged, in the name of Jesus.

13. Every demonic yoke upon my Destiny, break into pieces, in the name of Jesus.

14. Oh Lord, destroy every evil investment against my Destiny, in the name of Jesus.

DAY 65

Joel 2:12-17

Oh Lord, Awake My Destiny

1. Let my Destiny begin to swim in the river of the waters of life, in the name of Jesus.

2. Oh Lord, my God, take over my Destiny by fire, in the name of Jesus.

3. Any sacrifice offered against my Destiny, expire, in the name of Jesus.

4. I come against all the attackers of my destiny, in the name of Jesus.

5. Let the occultic organizations against my life scatter, in the name of Jesus.

6. Let the hosts of heaven begin to fight for me, in the name of Jesus.

7. Oh Lord, satisfy my Destiny with the riches of the gentiles, in the name of Jesus.

8. Everything on earth, fighting against my Destiny, fall down and die, in the name of Jesus.

9. Every strange voice, speaking against my Destiny, fall down and die, in the name of Jesus.

10. Let the dew of heaven fall upon my Destiny, in the name of Jesus.

11. Every strange God in my Destiny, you are wicked, therefore, die, in the name of Jesus.

12. Every earthly power in agreement against my Destiny, fall down and die, in the name of Jesus.

13. Blood of Jesus, speak peace into the foundation of my Destiny, in the name of Jesus.

14. Any power quenching the fire of God in my Destiny, die, in the name of Jesus.

DAY 66

Joel 2:12-17

Oh Lord, Awake My Destiny

1. Power of dryness against my Destiny, die, in the name of Jesus.

2. Blood of Jesus, frustrate the enemies of my Destiny, in the name of Jesus.

3. Every ancient landmark, tormenting my Destiny, be eliminated, in the name of Jesus.

4. Let the advancement of the enemy against my Destiny be terminated, in the name of Jesus.

5. Oh Lord, use everything you have created to set my Destiny free from captivity, in the name of Jesus.

6. Any power that is specialized in captivating destinies, in my family, collapse and die in the name of Jesus.

7. Blood of Jesus, attack my attackers, in the name of Jesus.

8. Oh Lord, take my Destiny away from every evil grip or chain, in the name of Jesus.

9. Oh Lord those answers by fire, answer me now, in the name of Jesus.

10. Divine nature of God; possess my Destiny by fire, in the name of Jesus.

11. My Destiny, your peace has come, arise by fire, in the name of Jesus.

12. You, my Destiny, hear the word of Christ now, in the name of Jesus.

13. Let the word of God rule and reign over my Destiny, in the name of Jesus.

14. Every divination of the wicked against my Destiny, backfire, in the name of Jesus.

DAY 67

Joel 2:12-17

Oh Lord, Awake My Destiny

1. I reject every satanic programme against my Destiny, in the name of Jesus.

2. Every satanic roadmap against my destiny, be disorganized, in the name of Jesus.

3. As the Lord liveth, my Destiny shall prosper, in the name of Jesus.

4. Oh Lord, destroy all manner of barrenness in my life, in the name of Jesus.

5. You the destroyer of my destiny, die, in the name of Jesus.

6. Any evil that took place against my Destiny between the hours of 12 midnight and 3 am, die, in the name of Jesus.

7. You this day, cooperate with my Destiny, in the name of Jesus.

8. Any satanic armed robber against my Destiny, be arrested, in the name of Jesus.

9. All evil powers must bow down to my destiny, in the name of Jesus.

10. This week must cooperate with my Destiny, in the name of Jesus.

11. All my unborn dreams must be born today, in the name of Jesus.

12. Any evil voice from hell must bow to the voice of my Destiny, in the name of Jesus.

13. Let all evil character that have arrested my Destiny release him now, in the name of Jesus.

14. You, power that quickened the dead, quicken my Destiny, in the name of Jesus.

DAY 68

Joel 2:12-17

Oh Lord, awake my Destiny

1. My environmental bewitchment shall not affect me, in the name of Jesus.

2. Every satanic desire against my destiny shall be frustrated, in the name of Jesus.

3. Divine warriors, arise and deliver my Destiny in the name of Jesus.

4. Let my Destiny appear and intimidate my problems in the name of Jesus.

5. Any power, keeping my Destiny in darkness, what are you waiting for? Die, in the name of Jesus.

6. Let the power suppressing my Destiny, die, in the name of Jesus.

7.   Every internal stronghold, built against my destiny, be broken by thunder, in the name of Jesus.

8.   You the satanic panel set against my destiny, be roasted by fire, in the name of Jesus.

9.   I replace my failures with divine success, in the name of Jesus.

10. Every fetish material directed, against my Destiny, die, in the name of Jesus.

11. Any satanic door into my Destiny, close by fire, in the name of Jesus.

12. Oh, Lord visits my Destiny and deliver me from destruction, in the name of Jesus.

13. I receive the divine anointing to kill my Destiny enemies, in the name of Jesus

14. You, my destiny, begin to change for the better, in the name of Jesus.

DAY 69

Joel 2:12-17

Oh Lord, Awake My Destiny

1. Every effort of the enemy, targeted against my Destiny, be wasted, in the name of Jesus.

2. Spirit of abortion, possess the powers of darkness against my marriage, in the name of Jesus.

3. You, the drinkers of blood and the eaters of flesh against my destiny, die immediately in the name of Jesus.

4. Every Sanballat and Tobiah against my Destiny, fall down and die, in the name of Jesus.

5. Every evil invitation handed on to my Destiny; I reject you by fire, in the name of Jesus.

6. Every embarrassment, following me up and down, perish by fire, in the name of Jesus.

7.   Father Lord, begin to promote my Destiny in the name of Jesus.

8.   Every evil dedication against my destiny, I renounce you, in the name of Jesus.

9.   I release my Destiny from every satanic bondage, in the name of Jesus.

10. You hands and legs of evil people in my destiny, be removed by force, in the name of Jesus.

11. Any witchcraft animal searching for my Destiny, die without success, in the name of Jesus.

12. Let the reviving power of God possess my Destiny, in the name of Jesus.

13. Angels of the living God, arise and deliver my Destiny, in the name of Jesus.

14. Oh Lord, arise and give my Destiny unimaginable promotion, in the name of Jesus.

DAY 70

Joel 2:12-17

Oh Lord, Awake My Destiny

1. Oh Lord, touch the life of my Destiny by fire, in the name of Jesus.

2. Every cloud of darkness against my Destiny, disappear, in the name of Jesus.

3. I remove my Destiny from the path of destruction and death, in the name of Jesus.

4. Any power sitting upon my promotion, be unseated, in the name of Jesus.

5. Every satanic cobweb blocking my way, receive fire and burn to ashes, in the name of Jesus.

6. Every stubborn darkness against my destiny, be removed by the thunder fire of God, in the name of Jesus.

7. Oh Lord, let your peace in my Destiny swallow every trouble in my life in the name of Jesus.

8. Oh Lord, examine my life and deliver my Destiny, in the name of Jesus.

9. Any power ready to arrest my Destiny, you are wicked; therefore, die, in the name of Jesus.

10. All satanic kingdoms raised against my Destiny, crumble into pieces, in the name of Jesus.

11. Oh Lord, anoint me with the holy oil, in the name of Jesus.

12. Every demonic alteration against my destiny, I reject you, in the name of Jesus.

13. Any evil power sitting upon my promotion, be unseated by death, in the name of Jesus.

14. Every curse placed upon my Destiny, die by fire, in the name of Jesus.

DAY 71

Daniel 10:1-3.13

Oh Lord, Awake My Destiny

1. Oh Lord, guide my decision by fire, in the name of Jesus.

2. Oh Lord, slap the enemies of my Destiny, in the name of Jesus.

3. Evil yoke placed upon my Destiny, be broken, in the name of Jesus.

4. Any power inside the waters, working against my Destiny, slump and die in the name of Jesus.

5. Every inherited problem in the root of my Destiny, be roasted by fire, in the name of Jesus.

6. You the spirit of worldliness, wasting my destiny, fall down and die, in the name of Jesus.

7. I dethrone every queen sitting in the waters of my destiny, fall down and die, in the name of Jesus.

8. Holy Ghost fire, charge the battle of my life in the name of Jesus.

9. I resign from satanic hard labor, in the name of Jesus.

10. I refuse to reveal the secret that will destroy my Destiny, in the name of Jesus.

11. Every effect of bewitchment against my Destiny, disappear, in the name of Jesus.

12. Thou evil manipulation of my destiny, die, in the name of Jesus.

13. Embargo of wickedness against my Destiny be lifted by force, in the name of Jesus.

14. My Destiny, refuse to manage poverty and defeats, in the name of Jesus.

DAY 72

Daniel 10:1-3, 13

Oh Lord, Awake My Destiny

1. Killer of miracles in my family line, die, in the name of Jesus.

2. My Destiny shall not serve his enemies, in the name of Jesus.

3. Any evil river, polluting my Destiny, dry up, in the name of Jesus.

4. I take away my greatness from the satanic prison, in the name of Jesus.

5. Fear will not destroy my Destiny, in the name of Jesus.

6. I reject every unprofitable reconciliation in the name of Jesus.

7. I refuse to be intimidated by water spirits, in the name of Jesus.

8. You my stubborn pursuers, fall down and die, in the name of Jesus.

9. I tear into pieces, all evil invitation letters designed to destroy me, in the name of Jesus.

10. I receive divine anointing to break the yokes of my life, in the name of Jesus.

11. You, the glory of God buried inside me, awake, in the name of Jesus.

12. Every confidence of the wicked against my Destiny, fail woefully, in the name of Jesus.

13. Every dream of backwardness against my Destiny, die, in the name of Jesus.

14. Oh Lord, remove my Destiny from every article of financial ruin, in the name of Jesus.

DAY 73

Daniel 10:1-3, 13

Oh Lord, Awake My Destiny

1. Oh Lord, let the mention of my name put terrible fears into the heart of my enemies, in the name of Jesus.

2. Every inherited limitation against my Destiny, disappear, in the name of Jesus.

3. You my tongue, speak death to my storms, in the name of Jesus.

4. Every evil establishment against my Destiny, scatter by divine whirlwind, in the name of Jesus.

5. I turn the sword of my Goliath against him, in the name of Jesus.

6. You the enemies of my Destiny, receive divine plagues, in the name of Jesus.

7. Oh Lord, show me where to cast my nets, in the name of Jesus.

8. Oh Lord, do not allow the good seed of my Destiny to die, in the name of Jesus.

9. Every spirit of evil tradition and custom fighting my Destiny, receive total rejection, in the name of Jesus.

10. You, spirit of fear and intimidation assigned to disgraced my Destiny, be disgraced, in the name of Jesus.

11. Every incurable disease in my blood vessels, die in the name of Jesus.

12. Every power of my father's house, die, in the name of Jesus.

13. Father Lord, take my Destiny to your desired result, in the name of Jesus.

14. Any witchcraft power against my Destiny, I reject you, in the name of Jesus.

DAY 74

Daniel 10:1-3, 13

Oh Lord, Awake My Destiny

1. You the moon of my Destiny, you shall not wane, in the name of Jesus.

2. My Destiny shall not continue in sorrow, in the name of Jesus.

3. Let the Lord arise mightily now for my Destiny, in the name of Jesus.

4. You, the Jericho of my Destiny, collapse, in the name of Jesus.

5. Every yoke of eating by the sweat of the face, be broken, in the name of Jesus.

6. Every hold of witchcraft working against my Destiny, be loosed in the name of Jesus.

7. Every deadly poison, prepared against my Destiny, expire in the name of Jesus.

8. Every spirit of unbelief, tormenting my Destiny, die, in the name of Jesus

9. My financial life, arise and shine forever, in the name of Jesus.

10. You my financial problem, receive healing, in the name of Jesus.

11. Any power sitting on my finances, be unseated by fire, in the name of Jesus.

12. Blood of Jesus, seal every door opened against my business, in the name of Jesus.

13. Oh, Lord give my Destiny uncommon success, in the name of Jesus.

14. By the wealthy name of Jesus, I deliver my Destiny from destruction, in the name of Jesus.

DAY 75

Daniel 10:1-3, 13

Oh Lord, Awake My Destiny

1. Holy Ghost fire, begin to arrest the spirit of poverty in my life, in the name of Jesus.

2. My Destiny will not labor for others in vain, in the name of Jesus.

3. Every poverty activator in my ministry, die, in the name of Jesus.

4. Divine success; overwhelm my Destiny, in the name of Jesus.

5. You, the strength of the emptiness, working against my Destiny, receive weakness by fire, in the name of Jesus.

6. You, my dead marriage, awake by force, in the name of Jesus.

7. You, my dead ministry, awake by fire, in the name of Jesus.

8. You, my dead health, awake by fire, in the name of Jesus.

9. You, my dead breakthroughs arise and shine for my Destiny, in the name of Jesus.

10. You, my angelic assistants, scatter the enemies of my Destiny, in the name of Jesus.

11. Holy Ghost fire, begin to arrest the spirit of death attacking my Destiny, in the name of Jesus.

12. You, spirit of deceit against my Destiny, die, in the name of Jesus.

13. Lord Jesus, promote my Destiny to the highest level in the name of Jesus.

14. Any evil power, causing scarcity in my Destiny, be disgraced by fire, in the name of Jesus.

DAY 76

Daniel 10:1-3, 13

Oh Lord, Awake My Destiny

1. Any spirit of strife against my Destiny, die, in the name of Jesus.

2. Spirit of mourning, destroying the good things of my life, die by force, in the name of Jesus.

3. Every arrow of unforgiving spirit fired into my life, I fire you back, in the name of Jesus.

4. My Destiny, refuse to turn back at the edge of breakthroughs, in the name of Jesus.

5. Oh Lord, plant every good thing upon my Destiny, in the name of Jesus.

6. You, the witchcraft arrow fired into my life, I fire you back, in the name of Jesus

7.   Rock of ages; gather my success together to your own glory, in the name of Jesus.

8.   Every arrow of depression against my Destiny backfire, backfire, backfire, in the name of Jesus.

9.   Any python that has swallowed my breakthroughs, die, in the name of Jesus.

10. Any satanic temple caging my finance, release them now, in the name of Jesus.

11. All satanic broadcasting stations talking against my ministry, be burnt completely, in the name of Jesus.

12. Whether the devil likes it or not, my Destiny shall awake, in the name of Jesus.

13. Let all the blessings that will make my Destiny great manifest, in the name of Jesus.

14. Father Lord, silence every satanic siren scaring my helpers, in the name of Jesus

DAY 77

Daniel 10:1-3, 13

Oh Lord, Awake My Destiny

1. I use the blood of Jesus to resurrect my dead Destiny, in the name of Jesus.

2. Every satanic attack against my marriage, cease by fire, in the name of Jesus.

3. I take authority over the marine powers attacking my Destiny, in the name of Jesus.

4. Let the glory of my destiny be brightened, in the name of Jesus.

5. Oh Lord, cause the sin of my Destiny to die forever, in the name of Jesus.

6. Oh Lord, heal my Destiny and restore my happiness, in the name of Jesus.

7. Father Lord, overturn the evil desires of marine powers against my Destiny, in the name of Jesus.

8. Every spiritual padlock holding my Destiny, break into pieces, in the name of Jesus.

9. Every evil domination and bondage against my destiny, be rejected, in the name of Jesus.

10. Let spirit of wolves working against my destiny, receive divine verdict, in the name of Jesus.

11. Any power, blocking my Destiny from entering into its promised land, die by fire, in the name of Jesus.

12. Any marine spirit seduction against my Destiny, die, in the name of Jesus.

13. Every witchcraft power, working against my Destiny, be destroyed, in the name of Jesus.

14. My Destiny, let harvest overtake harvest in you, in the name of Jesus.

DAY 78

Daniel 10:1-3, 13

Oh Lord, Awake My Destiny Stop

1. My Destiny shall not be trapped in the fowler's net, in the name of Jesus.

2. Any spirit of death, pursing my Destiny, be crippled, in the name of Jesus

3. Anything representing my Destiny on any evil altar, be roasted by fire, in the name of Jesus.

4. Every satanic attention against my destiny, be diverted, in the name of Jesus.

5. Father Lord, take me to the city of solutions, in the name of Jesus.

6. I break every ungodly tie that would destroy my Destiny, in the name of Jesus.

7. My Destiny shall not be shaken by the enemy, in the name of Jesus.

8. Every death contractor against my Destiny, kill your sender, in the name of Jesus.

9. I release my Destiny from every agent of sickness against it, in the name of Jesus.

10. Father Lord, disappoint every agent of sickness against my Destiny, in the name of Jesus.

11. All ye dead organs in my body, receive life, in the name of Jesus.

12. Every evil manipulation against my Destiny, be rejected by fire, in the name of Jesus.

13. Every witchcraft weapon assigned to waste my Destiny, be wasted, in the name of Jesus.

14. Every evil word of death spoken against my Destiny, backfire, in the name of Jesus.

DAY 79

Daniel 10:1-3, 13

Oh Lord, Awake My Destiny

1. Every spirit fertilizing infertility and fear, release me now, in the name of Jesus.

2. Any evil power standing against my Destiny and me, be destroyed by fire, in the name of Jesus.

3. Anointing to pray until my Destiny is delivered, possess me now, in the name of Jesus.

4. Any strange woman militating against my Destiny, you are wicked; die, in the name of Jesus.

5. All the legal right of my destiny stolen by Satan, be release by fire, in the name of Jesus.

6. Holy Ghost Fire, visit the foundation of my marital life, in the name of Jesus.

7. Any demonic incision affecting my destiny, die, in the name of Jesus.

8. Thou rod of the wicked, rising up against my Destiny, be rendered impotent, in the name of Jesus.

9. Any evil wall, blocking the sunlight of my Destiny, be dispersed by thunder, in the name of Jesus.

10. Any evil stone, holding my Destiny, be rolled away, in the name of Jesus.

11. All you evil spirits planning to trouble my Destiny, scatter by fire, in the name of Jesus.

12. Let my Destiny be too dangerous to be manipulated, in the name of Jesus.

13. Every witchcraft bungalow, built against my Destiny, collapse, in the name of Jesus.

14. Every fire of the enemy, assigned to burn my Destiny, quench, in the name of Jesus.

DAY 80

Daniel 10:1-3, 13

Oh Lord, Awake My Destiny

1. Any evil leg, standing upon my Destiny, be crippled, in the name of Jesus.

2. Every organized enemy from the water against my health and marriage, scatter, in the name of Jesus.

3. Thou evil demonic influence against my Destiny, die by fire, in the name of Jesus.

4. All demonic mirrors monitoring my destiny, break in the wall of fire, in the name of Jesus.

5. All the soiled part of my destiny, receive deliverance, in the name of Jesus.

6. You, the shame and the disappointment of my enemies, increase, in the name of Jesus.

7. Let my Destiny become coals of fire against the seed of iniquity, in the name of Jesus.

8. You the joy and boldness of my Destiny, be multiplied, in the name of Jesus.

9. Oh Lord, bless me beyond measure, in the name of Jesus.

10. Father Lord, do not shut my Destiny, in the name of Jesus.

11. All you appointed helpers of my Destiny, begin to locate me, in the name of Jesus.

12. All you my weakening glory, receive life, in the name of Jesus.

13. Every stubborn arrow holding my Destiny down, disappear, in the name of Jesus.

14. Every throne of the devil working against my Destiny, scatter, in the name of Jesus.

DAY 81

Ezekiel 18:21-23

Oh Lord, awake My Destiny

1. I reject every satanic inspiration targeted against my Destiny, in the name of Jesus.

2. I release my Destiny from every attack of poverty, in the name of Jesus.

3. I release my destiny from every curse of witchcraft, in the name of Jesus.

4. Every judgment passed against my Destiny, be reversed, in the name of Jesus.

5. Every good thing my Destiny has lost, I recover you double, in the name of Jesus.

6. Every garment of lack upon my Destiny, catch fire, in the name of Jesus.

7. I break and lose my Destiny from every curse of evil dedication, in the name of Jesus.

8.   Let the sword of fire begin to cut off every evil parental attachment affecting my Destiny, in the name of Jesus.

9.   Every anti progress spirit against my Destiny, die, in the name of Jesus.

10. Blood of Jesus, flow into the grave of my Destiny, in the name of Jesus.

11. 11. I vandalize and destroy all evil altars in my place of birth, in the name of Jesus.

12. Let all satanic agents circulating my name for evil be terminated, in the name of Jesus.

13. Strength and health from God, possess my Destiny, in the name of Jesus.

14. Every satanic programme, assigned to cage my Destiny, fail woefully, in the name of Jesus.

DAY 82

Ezekiel 18:21-23

Oh Lord, Awake My Lord

1. I release my Destiny from every curse of sickness, in the name of Jesus.

2. I release my marriage from every curse of failure and defeat, in the name of Jesus.

3. I release my business from every curse of profitless hard work, in the name of Jesus.

4. I command any evil spirit attached to my Destiny to depart immediately, in the name of Jesus.

5. I release my great Destiny from every curse of chronic sickness, in the name of Jesus.

6. I release my Destiny from every curse of chronic problems, in the name of Jesus.

7. I set my Destiny free from every curse of satanic oppression, in the name of Jesus.

8. I release my Destiny from every curse of marine control, in the name of Jesus.

9. I release my ministry from every curse of Pentecostal witchcraft attacks, in the name of Jesus.

10. I release my destiny from every curse of family strife, in the name of Jesus.

11. You my Destiny, receive deliverance from every curse of mental and physical sickness, in the name of Jesus.

12. I set my family free from every curse of family breakup, in the name of Jesus.

13. I release my ministry and career from any curse of bad reputation, in the name of Jesus.

14. Oh Lord, deliver my Destiny from every curse of personal destruction or suicide, in the name of Jesus.

DAY 83

Ezekiel 18:21-23

Oh Lord, Awake My Destiny

1. I recover the fullness of my joy from the captivity of marine powers, in the name of Jesus.

2. Blood of Jesus, deliver my Destiny from the consequences of parental curses, in the name of Jesus.

3. Holy Ghost fire, separate me from demonic marriage, in the name of Jesus.

4. My Destiny shall not be polluted by dream attackers, in the name of Jesus.

5. Oh Lord, do not permit the enemy to alter my destiny, in the name of Jesus.

6. Let the spirit of polygamy lose hold over my life, in the name of Jesus.

7.   I reject all the evil effects of inherited infirmity, in the name of Jesus.

8.   Oh Lord, deliver my Destiny from the attacks coming from my family idols, in the name of Jesus.

9.   I withdraw my Destiny from marine altars, in the name of Jesus.

10.   Anything representing me in any satanic temple, be roasted by fire, in the name of Jesus

11.   All the blessings of my Destiny on any evil altar, I withdraw you by fire, in the name of Jesus

12.   Any evil hand raised against my Destiny, dry up by fire, in the name of Jesus

13.   Oh Lord, release my destiny from every curse of evil dedication, in the name of Jesus

14.   I take back all that my ancestors have handed over to Satan, in the name of Jesus.

DAY 84

Ezekiel 18:21-23

Oh Lord, Awake My Destiny

1. You the glory of my Destiny on any evil altar, come out by fire, in the name of Jesus

2. 2 My prosperity shall not be wasted on any evil altar, in the name of Jesus

3. Every evil authority on any evil altar against my Destiny, die immediately, in the name of Jesus

4. I withdraw my Destiny from the bondage of sexual perversion, in the name of Jesus

5. I recover all the grounds I have lost to Satan through the sale of my virginity, in the name of Jesus.

6. I recover all the grounds I have lost to the enemy through idolatry, in the name of Jesus.

7. I recover all the grounds I have lost to the enemy through abortion, in the name of Jesus

8. Every association of my Destiny with witchcraft in the past, break by fire, in the name of Jesus.

9. Fire of God, uproot and burn any disease or germ in my blood, in the name of Jesus.

10. Any spirit of mind blankness against my Destiny, I bind and render you to naught, in the name of Jesus.

11. Every spirit of mind dullness against my Destiny, I cast you out, in the name of Jesus.

12. I hold the blood of Jesus against the enemies of my Destiny, in the name of Jesus.

13. Any power assigned to attack my Destiny with poverty, die, in the name of Jesus.

14. Any bewitchment against my Destiny to forsake the true God, fail woefully, in the name of Jesus.

DAY 85

Ezekiel 18:21-23

Oh Lord, Awake My Destiny

1. Oh Lord, deliver my Destiny from the cursed land, in the name of Jesus.

2. Any satanic agent working against my Destiny, be disgraced, in the name of Jesus.

3. Any ancestral sin pursuing my Destiny, die, in the name of Jesus.

4. Any witchcraft curse placed upon my Destiny, disappear, in the name of Jesus

5. Any curse of spiritual ignorance against my Destiny, be roasted by fire, in the name of Jesus.

6. I destroy every curse of sickness in my Destiny, in the name of Jesus

7. You demon of financial destruction against my Destiny, die, in the name of Jesus.

8. Every curse of marital destruction against my Destiny, die by fire, in the name of Jesus.

9. Every curse of family destruction working against my destiny, fail woefully, in the name of Jesus.

10. I release my Destiny from any curse coming from any past and deliberate sinful acts, in the name of Jesus.

11. I reverse every curse of failure placed upon my Destiny, in the name of Jesus.

12. Oh Lord, command every sickness to health, in the name of Jesus.

13. Oh Lord, energize my Destiny to overcome all his enemies, in the name of Jesus.

14. Every demonic leprosy upon my Destiny, catch fire and burn to ashes in the name of Jesus.

DAY 86

Ezekiel 18:21-23

Oh Lord, Awake My Destiny

1. Blood of Jesus, convert every frustration to life fulfillment, in the name of Jesus.

2. You, the enemies of my destiny, receive destruction, in the name of Jesus.

3. Let the enemies of my Destiny fail woefully, in the name of Jesus.

4. Thunder and hailstones, fall upon the enemies of my Destiny, in the name of Jesus.

5. Any woman/man attached to my life to destroy my Destiny, die, in the name of Jesus.

6. Oh Lord, cause the habitation of my Pharaoh to become desolate, in the name of Jesus.

7.   Oh Lord, arise and scatter the enemies of my Destiny, in the name of Jesus.

8.   Oh Lord, show me the greatness of my Destiny, in the name of Jesus.

9.   I reject every bewitchment, fashioned against my Destiny, in the name of Jesus.

10. Every covenant of marital failure in my place of birth, die now, in the name of Jesus.

11. Oh Lord, move the hand of household wickedness from my Destiny, in the name of Jesus.

12. Father Lord, let wonderful changes begin to take place in my destiny, in the name of Jesus.

13. Every uncleanness attached to my Destiny; receive divine cleansing, in the name of Jesus.

14. Father Lord, arise in your power and take my Destiny to the Promised Land, in the name of Jesus.

DAY 87

Ezekiel 18:21-23

Oh Lord, Awake My Destiny

1. I sever my Destiny from any satanic linkage and marine powers, in the name of Jesus.

2. I declare my Destiny free from the powers of the Egyptians, in the name of Jesus.

3. Oh Lord, do not let my Destiny share anything with the water spirits, in the name of Jesus.

4. Every mountain of impossibility against my Destiny, be dashed into pieces, in the name of Jesus.

5. My Destiny shall not reap an evil harvest, in the name of Jesus.

6. Let my Destiny become a terror to the powers of darkness, in the name of Jesus.

7. Any evil personality that will attack my Destiny shall die, in the name of Jesus.

8. You, the sun of my Destiny, be brightened, in the name of Jesus.

9. Every evil imagination against my Destiny, backfire, in the name of Jesus.

10. Let fire of God begin to destroy all the enemies of my Destiny, in the name of Jesus.

11. Father Lord, expose and disgrace all evil powers against my Destiny, in the name of Jesus.

12. Oh Lord, soak my Destiny in the pool of the blood of Jesus, in the name of Jesus.

13. Lord Jesus, anoint seventy elders to work with the Moses of my Destiny, in the name of Jesus.

14. Every tree of death planted against my Destiny, be uprooted, in the name of Jesus.

DAY 88

Ezekiel 18:21-23

Oh Lord, Awake My Destiny

1. I release death upon all the enemies of my Destiny, in the name of Jesus

2. I weaken the powers of the grave holding my Destiny, in the name of Jesus.

3. Spirit of death, leave my Destiny alone, in the name of Jesus.

4. Every issue of my Destiny, I take you away from the satanic register, in the name of Jesus.

5. All you enemies of my Destiny, gather yourselves together and destroy yourselves, in the name of Jesus.

6. All demonic communications into the secret affairs of my Destiny, be broken, in the name of Jesus.

7.   Oh Lord, convert my Destiny to your battle-axe, in the name of Jesus.

8.   Father Lord, add favor to the work of my Destiny, in the name of Jesus.

9.   Any satanic agenda against my Destiny, backfire, in the name of Jesus.

10. My Destiny will never die prematurely, in the name of Jesus.

11. Every satanic disease against my Destiny, be revoked now, in the name of Jesus.

12. Father Lord, bulldoze the way of my Destiny to divine breakthroughs, in the name of Jesus.

13. Any Dathan, Korah and Abiram raised against my Destiny, be disgraced, in the name of Jesus.

14. Let the personalities against my Destiny catch the Holy Ghost fire, in the name of Jesus.

DAY 89

Ezekiel 18:21-23

Oh Lord, Awake My Destiny

1.   Every yoke of unfaithfulness placed upon my Destiny, break by fire, in the name of Jesus

2.   Any satanic timetable against my Destiny, catch fire, in the name of Jesus.

3.   Let the great healing powers of God possess my Destiny, in the name of Jesus.

4.   Let the satanic deposit upon my Destiny be roasted by fire, in the name of Jesus

5.   Every deception, targeted against my Destiny, backfire, in the name of Jesus.

6.   Father Lord, guard my Destiny against evil diversion, in the name of Jesus.

7.   You, my Destiny, vomit every satanic poison, in the name of Jesus.

8.   All you satanically inspired prayers against my Destiny, backfire, in the name of Jesus.

9.   You, the eagle of my Destiny, fly, fly, and fly, in the name of Jesus.

10.   My entire buried destiny, come alive, in the name of Jesus.

11.   Every root cause of my buried Destiny, be exposed, in the name of Jesus.

12.   Any satanic angel attacking my Destiny, die, in the name of Jesus.

13.   Let the goodness of God rest upon my Destiny by fire, in the name of Jesus.

14.   Any judgment of death placed upon my Destiny, be reversed, in the name of Jesus.

DAY 90

Ezekiel 18:21-23

Oh Lord, Awake My Destiny

1. Oh Lord, bring light into the dark rooms of my Destiny, in the name of Jesus.

2. Any power, diverting the blessing of my Destiny, die, in the name of Jesus.

3. Father Lord, let your purpose for my Destiny be fulfilled today, in the name of Jesus.

4. Any satanic vulture, attacking my Destiny, die by fire, in the name of Jesus.

5. You, the unrepentant enemies of my Destiny, I burn you alive, in the name of Jesus.

6. Oh Lord, replace the weakness of my Destiny with divine strength, in the name of Jesus.

7. You, the blood of my Destiny, be purified, in the name of Jesus.

8. All worldly spirits of my Destiny, disappear, in the name of Jesus.

9. Every satanically inspired prayer against my life, backfire, in the name of Jesus

10. Every satanically prophecy against my life, backfire, in the name of Jesus.

11. Every satanically inspired speech against my life, backfire, in the name of Jesus.

12. Every satanically inspired speech against my Destiny, backfire, in the name of Jesus.

13. I command my Destiny to arise and laugh last, in the name of Jesus.

14. Any power assigned to cause my Destiny to backslide, fail woefully, in the name of Jesus.

DAY 91

Mathew 4:1, 2, 14:19-21

Oh Lord, awake my Destiny

1. Every satanically inspired fasting against my Destiny, be reversed, in the name of Jesus.

2. Every satanically inspired action against my Destiny, be reversed, in the name of Jesus.

3. Every satanically inspired programme against my Destiny, be reversed, in the name of Jesus.

4. Every satanically inspired journey against my Destiny, be terminated, in the name of Jesus.

5. Every satanically inspired access into my Destiny, be closed up, in the name of Jesus.

6. Every fake friend, attached to my Destiny, die, in the name of Jesus.

7. Holy Spirit, help me to know all that I am supposed to know, in the name of Jesus.

8. Let the agent of frustration against my Destiny die, in the name of Jesus.

9. Every satanic inspired speech against my life, backfire, in the name of Jesus.

10. I reject any partial deliverance to my Destiny, in the name of Jesus.

11. Let all my oppressors be oppressed by fire, in the name of Jesus.

12. All evil hosts against my Destiny, scatter, in the name of Jesus.

13. Any evil oppressor against my Destiny, be oppressed unto death, in the name of Jesus.

14. Any Achan about to destroy my Destiny be disgraced in the public, in the name of Jesus.

DAY 92

Matthew 4:1, 2, 14:19-21

Oh Lord, Awake My Destiny

1. Any personal invitation I have given to the enemies of my Destiny, I withdraw you now, in the name of Jesus.

2. You my Destiny, become an instrument of divine prosperity, in the name of Jesus.

3. Lord Jesus, catapult my Destiny to the mountaintop, in the name of Jesus.

4. My Destiny, reject the life of the valley, climb the mountaintop, in the name of Jesus.

5. Any evil marriage prolonging my bondage, break by fire, in the name of Jesus.

6. I break the powers of any demonic appeal issued against my Destiny, in the name of Jesus.

7.   The deliverance of my Destiny must be complete and not partial, in the name of Jesus.

8.   Blood of Jesus, erase every mark upon my Destiny, in the name of Jesus.

9.   The spirit of self-termination shall not terminate my Destiny, in the name of Jesus.

10. Any agent of demonic delays, fashioned against my Destiny, die in the name of Jesus.

11. Oh Lord, trouble all the troubles of my Destiny, in the name of Jesus.

12. I claim divine wisdom that will promote my Destiny, in the name of Jesus.

13. Every satanic embargo placed upon my foundation, be lifted, in the name of Jesus.

14. Let the sum of my destiny stand still until my Destiny is delivered, in the name of Jesus.

DAY 93

Mathew 4:1, 2, 14:19-21

Oh Lord, Awake My Destiny

1. Father Lord, quicken my dead account, in the name of Jesus.

2. Father Lord, resurrect all my dead organs, in the name of Jesus.

3. I conquer every spirit of fear upon my Destiny, in the name of Jesus.

4. I issue destructive judgment against the marine powers attacking my Destiny, in the name of Jesus.

5. You, my shoulder, reject every evil load, in the name of Jesus.

6. I drink the blood of Jesus for divine energy against marine powers, in the name of Jesus.

7.   I release my Destiny from the domination and control of failure, in the name of Jesus.

8.   Oh Lord, give my Destiny complete liberty, in the name of Jesus.

9.   You, the spirits of my town and village, release my Destiny by fire, in the name of Jesus.

10. I bind the strongman troubling my Destiny, in the name of Jesus.

11. Evil worms in the brain of my Destiny, die, in the name of Jesus.

12. Every serpent, set in motion against my Destiny, bite your sender and die, in the name of Jesus.

13. Lord Jesus, strengthen my Destiny to fight unto victory, in the name of Jesus.

14. Every conspiracy against my Destiny, be exposed and be disgraced, in the name of Jesus.

DAY 94

Ezekiel 18:21-23

Oh Lord, Awake My Destiny

1.   Every evil design against my Destiny, die, in the name of Jesus.

2.   Every strongman in charge of my business, you are wicked; therefore, die, in the name of Jesus.

3.   Holy Ghost fire, incubate my health, in the name of Jesus.

4.   All you evil mountains, break your powers over my Destiny, in the name of Jesus.

5.   Oh Lord, shield my Destiny away from all deception, in the name of Jesus.

6.   Let the light of God illuminate the graveyard of my Destiny, in the name of Jesus.

7.   Every darkness upon my Destiny, begin to see clearly, in the name of Jesus.

8. Oh Lord, wash the brain of my Destiny by fire, in the name of Jesus.

9. I cut down the powers of transitional forces working against my Destiny, in the name of Jesus.

10. Oh Lord, let me see what will happen to the enemies of my Destiny this week, in the name of Jesus.

11. I divorce every satanic husband/wife against my destiny, in the name of Jesus.

12. Every evil stone thrown at my Destiny, backfire, in the name of Jesus.

13. Let my helpless Destiny receive divine help from above, in the name of Jesus.

14. Any power, delegated against my Destiny by my father's idol, die, in the name of Jesus.

DAY 95

Matthew 4:1, 2, 14:19-21

Oh Lord, Awake My Destiny

1. There shall be no negotiation, dialogue or agreement with the enemies of my Destiny, in the name of Jesus.

2. Fire of God, visit all the homes of witches and wizards and recover my Destiny, in the name of Jesus.

3. I block every satanic entrance into my life, in the name of Jesus.

4. You, my Destiny, receive power to overcome every obstacle, in the name of Jesus.

5. Witchcraft powers, depart, depart from my Destiny, in the name of Jesus.

6. I cut down by fire, every evil tree standing against my Destiny, in the name of Jesus.

7.   Father Lord, re-arrange the destiny of my life to your taste, in the name of Jesus.

8.   Oh Lord, let your healing power take firm roots within my body, soul and spirit, in the name of Jesus.

9.   Every contrary force against my Destiny, die by fire, in the name of Jesus.

10.   I fire back every arrow of witchcraft against my Destiny, in the name of Jesus.

11.   Holy Ghost power, deliver my Destiny from the trouble city, in the name of Jesus.

12.   I send the fire of God to heal my hormonal imbalance or other secretions in my body, in the name of Jesus.

13.   Any tribal spirit waiting to attack my Destiny, be frustrated, in the name of Jesus.

14.   Heavenly Father, lift every area of my Destiny, in the name of Jesus.

DAY 96

Matthew 4:1, 2, 14:19-21

Oh Lord, Awake My Destiny

1. Blood of Jesus, Holy Ghost fire, heal my brain and set my Destiny free, in the name of Jesus.

2. Father Lord, add more fire to my Destiny, in the name of Jesus.

3. All anti miracle spirits against my destiny, die by fire, in the name of Jesus.

4. Any satanic rumor fashioned against my destiny, be silenced, in the name of Jesus.

5. I stand against any careless word against my Destiny, in the name of Jesus.

6. Oh Lord, arise and let my Destiny be promoted, in the name of Jesus.

7. Every pocket of my Destiny with evil holes, close now, in the name of Jesus.

8. Oh Lord my God, retrieve all my blessings from the covens of marine powers, in the name of Jesus.

9. Father Lord, increase my joy and advertise satanic defeats, in the name of Jesus.

10. Oh, Lord, break the teeth of the ungodly gathered against my Destiny, in the name of Jesus.

11. Every satanic satellite and camera, monitoring my Destiny, be broken by fire, in the name of Jesus.

12. Powers from the third heaven, recover my Destiny from the grave, in the name of Jesus.

13. Any evil investment against my Destiny, catch fire, in the name of Jesus.

14. Every strange voice speaking against my Destiny, be silenced, in the name of Jesus.

DAY 97

Matthew 4:1, 2, 14:19-21

Oh Lord, Awake My Destiny

1. Every satanic connection to my Destiny, break by fire, in the name of Jesus.

2. Every handwriting of the enemy against my Destiny, be reversed, in the name of Jesus.

3. Father Lord, cause me to celebrate my deliverance, in the name of Jesus.

4. Oh Lord, pump your power of victory into my Destiny, in the name of Jesus.

5. Any satanic impurity in my Destiny, be flushed out by fire, in the name of Jesus.

6. Any satanic kingdom after my Destiny, I destroy you by thunder, in the name of Jesus.

7.   All the armors and the weapons of my family strongman, I destroy you now, in the name of Jesus.

8.   Father Lord, begin to speak to my Destiny, in the name of Jesus.

9.   You, my Destiny, come forth now, in the name of Jesus.

10. Lord, let your death substitute the death of my Destiny now, in the name of Jesus.

11. I damage all the powers of marine witchcraft working against my Destiny, in the name of Jesus.

12. You, the arrows of my prayers, enter into the marine kingdom now, in the name of Jesus.

13. My Destiny, arise and shine, in the name of Jesus.

14. I bind and cast out every demon assigned against my Destiny, in the name of Jesus.

DAY 98

Matthew 4:1, 2, 14:19-21

Oh Lord, Awake My Destiny

1. Every environmental problem pursuing my Destiny, receive destruction, in the name of Jesus.

2. Every satanic parasite eating the strength of my Destiny, die immediately, in the name of Jesus.

3. You the stones of my prayers, kill my Goliath today, in the name of Jesus.

4. Every satanic animal in the bush of my life, die and die again, in the name of Jesus.

5. Father Lord, promote my Destiny forever, in the name of Jesus.

6. Oh Lord, renovate the powers of my Destiny, in the name of Jesus.

7. Let that force that wastes Destiny die now, in the name of Jesus.

8. Father Lord, give me the grace to recover all the grounds I have lost, in the name of Jesus.

9. My Destiny, be transported from minimum to maximum, in the name of Jesus.

10. Satan, touch not my anointed Destiny and do him no attacks; attack yourselves, in the name of Jesus.

11. Father Lord, begin to do that which is necessary to promote my Destiny, in the name of Jesus.

12. I fire back every household witchcraft arrows, in the name of Jesus.

13. You the Delilah and jezebel with a vow to kill my Destiny, die by fire, in the name of Jesus.

14. All the stolen promotions of my Destiny, I recover you, in the name of Jesus.

DAY 99

Matthew 4:1, 2, 14:19-21

Oh Lord, Awake My Destiny

1. Let that power that killed Pharaoh arise and kill the Pharaoh of my brain, in the name of Jesus.

2. Let that power that destroyed Sodom and Gomorrah arise and repeat the work, in the name of Jesus.

3. I lose my Destiny from the bondage of fear and death, in the name of Jesus.

4. Every development against my Destiny, backfire, in the name of Jesus.

5. You, my Destiny, drop the garment of poverty today, in the name of Jesus.

6. Oh Lord, replace everything that needs replacement in my destiny, in the name of Jesus.

7.   I begin to understand the programmes of God for my Destiny, in the name of Jesus.

8.   Let every tree planted by the marine princes in my life be uprooted now, in the name of Jesus.

9.   Spirit of sleeplessness, you are wicked; therefore, die, die, die, in the name of Jesus.

10.   Just as you delivered Hezekiah, Oh God, deliver my Destiny from sickness, in the name of Jesus.

11.   You the barrenness of my Hannah, die, in the name of Jesus

12.   Every power of evil repetition in my life, die, in the name of Jesus.

13.   You my prayers, locate every anti-Destiny in my father's house and destroy it, in the name of Jesus.

14.   Fire of God, burn until the habitations of Sodom and Gomorrah are consumed, in the name of Jesus.

15.   You, my sleeping Destiny, awake to your glory, in the name of Jesus.

DAY 100

Matthew 4:1, 2, 14:19-21

Oh Lord, Awake My Destiny

1. You, the youth of my Destiny, be renewed by fire, in the name of Jesus.

2. My Destiny, box all your enemies to a corner, in the name of Jesus.

3. Let that oracle speaking against my Destiny be destroyed, in the name of Jesus.

4. Any python of darkness that has swallowed my Destiny vomit it and die, in the name of Jesus.

5. You, the health of my Destiny, it is your turn to shine, in the name of Jesus.

6. You, the town of my Destiny, be counted to Israel, in the name of Jesus.

7. Father Lord, let the cries of my Destiny reach your ears, in the name of Jesus.

8. You, my Destiny, refuse to enter into any satanic coffin, in the name of Jesus.

9. You, the mountains of my Destiny, be converted into dumb founding miracles, in the name of Jesus.

10. Let divine thunder destroy every altar constructed against my Destiny, in the name of Jesus.

11. Every evil pronouncement against my Destiny, backfire, in the name of Jesus.

12. Every chain of demonic agents against my destiny, break into pieces, in the name of Jesus.

13. You, hand of any evil priest, ministering against my Destiny, dry up by fire, in the name of Jesus.

14. Any satanic lion assigned to kill my Daniel, you are a failure; kill your sender, in the name of Jesus.

15. Every seed of destruction in the foundation of my Destiny, die, in the name of Jesus.

THANK YOU!

I'd like to use this time to thank you for purchasing my books and helping my ministry and work. Any copy of my book you buy helps to fund my ministry and family, as well as offering much-needed inspiration to keep writing. My family and I are very thankful, and we take your assistance very seriously.

You have already accomplished so much, but I would appreciate an honest review of some of my books through the link below. This is critical since reviews reflect how much an author's work is respected.

Please [click here] to leave a review on Amazon. If you're viewing from a printed version, please visit amazon.com/review/create-review?asin=B0892678RK to leave a review.

Please be aware that I read and value all comments and reviews. You can always post a review even though you haven't finished the book yet, and then edit your reviews later.

Thank you so much as you spare a precious moment of your time and may God bless you and meet you at the very point of your need.

You can also send me an email to hello@madueke.com if you encounter any difficulty while writing your review.

PRAYER M. MADUEKE'S BESTSELLING BOOKS

Click on any of the [Buy Now] buttons to view or purchase them on my website. If you're viewing from a printed version, please visit madueke.com and search for these books.

1. Dictionary of Demons & Complete Deliverance — [Buy Now]

2. Monitoring Spirits — [Buy Now]

3. Praying with The Blood of Jesus — [Buy Now]

4. The Power of Speaking in Tongues — [Buy Now]

5. Speaking Things into Existence by Faith — [Buy Now]

6. Discerning and Defeating the Ahab & Jezebel Spirit — [Buy Now]

7. Defeating the Python Spirit — [Buy Now]

8. 35 Special Dangerous Decrees — [Buy Now]

9. 21/40 Nights of Decrees and Your Enemies Will Surrender — [Buy Now]

23. When Evil Altars are Multiplied [**Buy Now**]

24. The Battle Plan for Destroying
    Foundational Occultism [**Buy Now**]

25. Prayers for Protection [**Buy Now**]

26. Prayers for Academic Success [**Buy Now**]

27. Your Dream Directory [**Buy Now**]

28. Prayers for Financial Breakthrough [**Buy Now**]

29. Destiny and Star Hunters [**Buy Now**]

30. Prayers to Pray during Courtship [**Buy Now**]

31. 91 Days Decrees to Takeover the Year [**Buy Now**]

32. Alone with God [**Buy Now**]

33. Prayers against Satanic Oppression [**Buy Now**]

34. Foundations Exposed [**Buy Now**]

35. Prayers for Deliverance [**Buy Now**]

36. Prayers to Heal Broken Relationship [**Buy Now**]

4 Free Ebooks

In order to say a 'Thank You' for purchasing *100 Days Prayers to Wake Up Your Lazarus*, I offer these books to you in appreciation. Click or type **madueke.com/free-gift** in your browser.

Video Bonus

I've created exclusive video content to complement the topics covered in the book. These videos provide deeper insights and discussions on the things discussed in this book, offering you a more immersive learning experience.

To access the video bonus for this course, simply click or type links.madueke.com/1DTP in your browser.

Message from the Author

I want to see you succeed, grow, and break free from negativity and obstacles. My hope is for you to thrive, unaffected by negative influences and challenging situations. Because of that, please permit me to introduce two courses that I believe passionately will help you:

1. To break the evil altars and powers of your father's house, The role of altars in the realm of existence is very key because altars are meeting places between the physical and the spiritual, between the visible and the invisible.

    Unless a man cuts off the evil flow from the power of his father's house, he will not fulfil his destiny. **Click here** to learn more about **my course** on how to tear down unholy altars and close the enemy's entryways into your life!

2. To help you seamlessly break iron-like problems, illness, delayed marriage, poverty, or any long-standing battle.

    Discover **the transformative power of Christian fasting and prayer**. Remember, Matthew 17:21 teaches us, *"But this kind of demon does not go out except by prayer and* *fasting."* Ready to overcome your struggles? <u>Click here</u> to learn more about this course.

Embrace the journey ahead with faith, for through prayer, fasting, and the dismantling of evil altars, you shall unlock the doors to spiritual liberation and divine breakthrough. May your path be illuminated by His grace as you walk towards a life free from bondage.

If you're seeing this from the physical copy, type the link: <u>madueke.com/courses</u> in your browser to view all the courses on my website.

Prayer Madueke
CHRISTIAN AUTHOR

Christian Counselling

We were created for a greater purpose than only survival and God wants us to live a full life.

If you need prayer or counselling, or if you have any other inquiries, please visit the counselling page on my website to know when I will be available for a phone call.

Click or type **links.madueke.com/counselling** in your browser.

Let's Connect on Youtube ▶

Join me on my YouTube channel, "Prayer M. Madueke," where I share powerful insights, guidance, and prayers for spiritual breakthroughs.

Subscribe today to unlock the secrets of the Kingdom and embrace an abundant life. Let's grow together!

Click or type **links.madueke.com/youtube** in your browser.

An Invitation to Become
a Ministry Partner

I appreciate the support and inquiries I have received regarding collaboration with my ministry. Your prayers and dedication to the work of the Kingdom are highly valued.

You can also visit the donation page on my website if you would like to contribute or learn more about supporting my ministry: madueke.com/donate.

Thank you for your continued support and faithfulness in Christ Jesus.